Praise for

Drunk, Divorced & Covered in Cat Hair

"She's absolutely, phenomenally hysterical!"

Modeknit.com

"I just have to say I love Crazy Aunt Purl (aka Laurie, lover of knitting, wine, and kitties). I am hardly the only one, though. Everyone seems to love her."

Divaknitting.com

"*Drunk, Divorced & Covered in Cat Hair* is—surprise—not just for women. A heart-wrenching mix of sadness and humor, any man who has experienced a broken heart will relate to the story of Laurie's divorce, the death of a marriage, and the reentry into single life. As men, we will not fully understand the humor of hair removal, perhaps, but her themes are resonant for all people, men and women, who've had love and loss and laughed in between."

Drew Emborsky, author of
Men Who Knit & the Dogs Who Love Them

"Poignant, funny, and something every woman will relate to, whether or not she's been divorced, whether or not she knits, whether or not she finds herself covered in cat hair 'from the knees down.' My only criticism—I didn't want it to end!"

Annie Modesitt, author of
Twist and Loop *and* Romantic Hand Knits

Drunk, Divorced & Covered in Cat Hair

Laurie Perry

Health Communications, Inc.
Deerfield Beach, Florida

www.hcibooks.com

Disclaimer: The events described in this book are true as I remember them, best as I could what with being covered in cat hair and three minutes from directing traffic in my nightgown. Some names and details have been changed, including the cats, even though they are always looking for their fifteen minutes of fame.

Library of Congress Cataloging-in-Publication Data

Perry, Laurie Beasley.
    Drunk, divorced & covered in cat hair : the true-life misadventures of a
       30-something who learned to knit after he split / Laurie Beasley Perry.
      p. cm.
    ISBN-13: 978-0-7573-0591-7 (trade paper)
    ISBN-10: 0-7573-0591-1 (trade paper)
    1. Perry, Laurie Beasley.   2. Divorced women—California—Los Angeles—
Biography.   3. Divorced women—California—Los Angeles—Psychology.
4. Divorced women—California—Los Angeles—Attitudes.   5. Divorce—United States
—Psychological aspects.   I. Title.   II. Title: Drunk, divorced, and covered in cat hair.

    HQ814.P46 2007
    306.89'3092—dc22

                   [B]
              2007016677

Publisher: Health Communications, Inc.
           3201 S.W. 15th Street
           Deerfield Beach, FL 33442-8190

Cover design by Andrea Perrine Brower
Interior design and formatting by Lawna Patterson Oldfield

This book is dedicated to my dad,
Larry Beasley, who is the glue holding
together my whole nutty Southern family.
Thanks for teaching me how to laugh,
Daddy, and sorry for all
the swear words.
I love you.

And to every single woman
who has ever been three minutes from crazy,
this book is for you. I've been there—
pass the wine.

Contents

Introduction

. . . .

A few months after my husband moved out, one of my best friends dragged me off to a knitting class. Frankly, I had no interest in knitting, and besides, I didn't want to leave the house. It was a Saturday, after all, and it was about to be five o'clock somewhere. But I went to this knitting class because my friend was concerned for my sanity and probably needed to see proof of life. That day, I learned the basics: how to cast on and how to make the knit stitch. And it took. Before long I was completely obsessed, knitting through sleepless nights and hours alone. I didn't knit because I needed a wool scarf for the coming Los Angeles winter or because I wanted to become a great knitter.

No.

I knitted because it kept my hands busy so I wouldn't drunk-dial my soon-to-be-ex-husband in an embarrassing and humiliating moment of weakness. I knitted through sixteen scarves, two hats, and one gigantic cat toy before the urge to pick up the phone had fully passed and by then . . . well, frankly, I was quite hooked on it.

Besides, as a knitter, you are armed at all times with two very sharp sticks, some sturdy string, and well-concealed scissors.

And that's a very comforting thing.

Part 1
Tightly Wound

Chapter 1

. . . .

𝒯𝒽𝑒𝓇𝑒 𝒶𝓇𝑒 𝓉𝒽𝓇𝑒𝑒 𝓇𝓊𝓁𝑒𝓈 every Southern girl has hammered into her consciousness, and they shape you and haunt you until the day you die.

Cardinal Rule Number One: **Mind your manners.**

This is of course the most important rule, especially early on in your upbringing, as it applies to everything from "watch your mouth" to "mind your elders," and encompasses all forms of behavior from "elbows off that table *rightnow*" to "do not look at me in that tone of voice." As you get on up in years you learn to mind your manners by not pitching a hissy fit when a smile and firm but pleasant tone will do, and by always being strong and kind, and of course you never smoke standing upright or while wearing your sorority pin. Because that is just tacky.

Cardinal Rule Number Two: **Make the best of a situation.**

When delivered by your Uncle Truman or a male teacher or your softball coach, this rule can sound like "Keep your chin up" or "Put your game face on." Sometimes there's a bait-and-switch approach, where you may have (in a moment of weakness) confessed some sad or upsetting thing to a willing human listener, and they reply back with a long, often horribly detailed story of the so-and-so girl who faces a far worse and more disastrous situation than you yourself could even imagine, which I suppose is meant to make you feel better about your own pathetic sob story but on me has the opposite effect.

Cardinal Rule Number Three: **Always wear clean panties.**

This particular gem was amended by my mother when I was sixteen, as she warned me in no uncertain terms to always wear clean panties *and keep them on.*

These rules presented for me a dilemma of decorum at the best of times and a true test of character at the worst of times. My comportment was once again in the crosshairs on the day this story begins, a day like any other, really, a completely normal day.

Although I was a married woman of thirty-three years of age living in cosmopolitan Los Angeles, California, and working in a downtown skyscraper (I work at a bank, but it sounds more glamorous to say *downtown skyscraper*), quite a remarkable departure from my small-town roots, I was now facing the trifecta of Southern Cardinal Rules, brought on by a rather strange and airy sensation in the back regions of my gray pinstripe skirt.

I felt a draft. *Back there.*

Today, the day of my inconvenient new rear-facing air-conditioning system, was a day of precarious underwear selection. While I had every intention of going home that very evening and facing Mount Washmore, the laundry pile in my bedroom closet, I was currently Making The Best Of Things. The wash-day panties I was wearing were nothing more than a string holding together some cotton, and not only was it an unfortunate thong-style contraption, it had the novelty of being green and red because I was on my Christmas undies. I had not embarked upon any lunchtime calisthenics, or lobbed kung fu kicks on my coffee break, or done anything, really, aside from sit on my ass in an air-conditioned office and Look Busy. Graphic designers at financial institutions do not have physically vexing jobs. But as soon as I stood up to stretch, I felt it—yes—a definite draft.

First I performed the not-so-subtle maneuver of slightly pulling my skirt to the left and craning my head back to see if I could spot the damage. Nothing.

A quick recon mission with my hands told me all I needed to know: my skirt had distinctly more air-conditioning in the backyard than it had this morning when I pulled it on. Sans panty hose. Meaning, at any moment my Christmas-themed underthings could be exposed to the cruel office air, in *August,* and also, this was maybe not the sort of impression I wanted my coworkers to have of me.

I stood in my cubicle and considered the alternatives. No sewing kit, so there's that. No safety pins either. I started for a moment toward the tape dispenser, but let's be honest here: no amount of Scotch tape in the world could keep my ample behind encased in pinstripes. So I did the only thing I could think of, and with my heavy black corporate stapler in hand, I crab-walked demurely through the hallway into the ladies' room. I moved pretty quickly considering all the wind rustling in the eaves behind me, desperately hoping not to run into any chatty or curious or *breathing* coworkers who might wonder why I had to take my stapler to the restroom with me.

I made it into the ladies' room without running into anyone, locked myself into the stall (the big one, of course, better for maneuvering), and stripped off my skirt to perform the necessary stapling surgery on the back seam.

One might imagine that sitting with staples up your backside for the rest of the workday would not be a particularly comfortable thing to do. One would be right. But that's what I did for the rest of that afternoon, squirming as little as possible, wondering if I were up-to-date on my tetanus shots, wondering if I could actually drink a glass of wine the size of my head when I got home, wondering if my mother had envisioned this very scenario when she advised keeping my panties on. I doubted it.

I drove home that night, a normal night like any other, tired, staples pressing into the backs of my thighs. It was a Thursday, and I sat in traffic trying to decide what to make me and my husband Charlie for dinner. Spaghetti? Baked chicken? Meat loaf? He had very particular tastes when it came to eating, nothing with sauce (except pasta), chunks, or garnishes. No salads and no vegetables besides fried or mashed potatoes, corn, green beans, and (surprisingly) peas. During the first year of our marriage this seemed unusually cruel for a new, young wife who couldn't cook.

"So you'll eat tomato sauce, like on pizza or pasta, but not *actual* tomatoes?"

"Yep."

"Fascinating."

Somewhere around year four, I rose to the challenge and began to see cooking as an experiment in creativity: what could I prepare, with my limited skills and his limited palate, that would be edible and also pass the Picky Test?

That night, I walked through the door, said hi to my husband, "Hey! Howwasyourday, I got staples in my behind, be right back," scratched a cat on the head, and stripped off my poor mangled skirt. I made dinner—spaghetti after all. Charlie liked it with extra Parmesan cheese sprinkled on top, and we sat eating it at the table on a Thursday night just like any other. And that is when my husband told me he was leaving.

And then he did.

And that is where this story begins.

Chapter 2

· ·

Charlie had a way of melting his whole face into putty, a wounded little-boy face of exaggerated innocence that could drive me to new levels of feral hysteria. When I wanted to speak to him about something, anything, any domestic issue, even something as simple as "I was wondering if you could help me clean the bathroom tomorrow . . . ," he went blank as a loaf of bread.

This evening was no different. He told me he was moving out—"I think it will be good for us . . . ," he said, in the exact same voice he would have used to suggest we run up to the store and get some ice—and as soon as I uttered a word contrary, he fixed his stare, held tight to his drink, and did what I can only imagine was his version of buckling in for the ride.

I begged him not to go, but he informed me he'd already found a bachelor apartment in another part of the city. His tone was still matter-of-fact, like the logistics of our separation were as easy and mundane as discussing the electric bill.

"I need to get my creativity back," he said.

"What does that mean? What have I done?"

Silence.

"I'll do whatever you want," I told him. Crying. Pathetic. "Just tell me how to fix what's wrong."

"I need to be free of responsibility," he said.

"I need you," I cried back. "Don't leave."

In the days that followed, I sat at the top of the steps and cried into the sleeve of my pajamas every night. By the week's end, I was sleeping in the guest bed on a twin-sized mattress with ugly pale-pink sheets. I hovered somewhere between mortal hurt and total insanity. The night before he moved out, we sat in the living room of the condo having what would be the last, very last, discussion on the subject at hand, that subject being my husband abandoning me and four cats in a cavernous house, in a scary city, in a world we'd promised to stand side by side in forever.

"Just tell me what it is, I'll fix it," I said. "You can get your creativity back here with me. I'll help you, I'll change. I can fix this, I know I can. . . . "

Because I was a *fixer*. I managed. I made the best of things. I kept my chin up. This was who I had always been, and I was just as sure I could fix this as anything, because commitment to a goal (no matter how wrong, sinful, unladylike, or frankly implausible the goal) was a character trait I had in spades.

He said nothing. I wondered what timbre of crazy I'd have to crank up to get him to hear me, see me, *for the love of God just listen.*

"Charlie?" I asked.

He just sat there. Bump on a goddamn log.

I realized in that very moment that even if I tore off into a new level of absurd—took the Saran Wrap from the kitchen cabinet and started systematically encasing everything in our lives in clear plastic: the sofa, the TV remote control, the toilet paper, Charlie himself, his cocktail glass, the suitcases he'd drawn out of the closet in an effort to prepare for his upcoming departure, the cats—I knew he would just sit there rigid as a stop sign and poke a hole in the plastic around his drink and sip quietly at his rum and Coke while I tried to freeze everything in the moment, to make us all incapable of moving forward or backward.

Nothing would keep him.

There was nothing to be done.

And that is a terrible place to be.

Chapter 3

· ·

Perhaps there is a fourth tenet of Southern upbringing: "Maybe you'd feel better if you ate something."

This one I've got down pat.

In the space of time between Charlie telling me he was leaving and the actual moving out, I managed to embrace this rule above all others. Some people, when faced with impending doom and chaotic instability, lose the ability to eat. I feel so sorry for these people. I am also, conversely, incredibly jealous of these rare creatures. I have always had a healthy appetite: even when I feel nauseated, perhaps after a long night of maudlin carrying on, I will wake up the next morning with acid pooling at the very pit of me and think, *My stomach is upset. I should probably eat something so I will feel better.*

And when I feel better, I think, *Since I'm feeling less paltry now, I should probably eat something! To keep my strength up, of course.* Usually it is something with cheese on it, or fried, or wrapped in bacon. These are sustaining foods for trying times.

Where I'm from, happy events are celebrated with food, but sadness is what brings out a true hunger. Southern funerals are well known for their wide assortment of cheese-covered casseroles

· · · · ·

and all sorts of creations topped with French's French Fried Onions, bread crumbs, or crushed cornflakes. You would be surprised at the large number of comforting casseroles that spring to mind when one is being jettisoned by her betrothed. You might also be amazed at how many things can be wrapped in a piece of bacon.

The loss of a husband came with a wide assortment of beverages, too: cabernet, pinot, Jack Daniel's out of a coffee cup. I am not sure why exactly, but I equate grief and sadness with drinking Jack Daniel's out of a coffee cup and eating Cheetos off my chest. Cheetos, mashed potatoes, macaroni and cheese, ice cream, anything with chocolate on it . . . nothing is better for numbing your soul than the sheer, unbridled love of the carbohydrate.

Eating is also a good way to keep your mouth busy so you don't say crazy things. There were times I would sit at my desk at work in the middle of the day and find myself on the verge of standing up and yelling, to no one in particular, "You suppose this creativity he's leaving me to pursue comes in a D cup? Wonder if this creativity of his has a name? *I wonder, oh yes I do!*" Instead, I ate a little snack at these precarious moments. To take the edge off, y'all understand.

The day he moved out, I was at work making spreadsheets and small talk with my coworkers. I had told no one that Charlie was leaving; it felt shameful, and I was terrified of saying the words out loud, making them real.

I had no idea what would happen to me. How would I support myself? Where would I live? Who would I be? Who was I, anyway? My entire identity was wrapped up in my role as wife and companion, something I became once my role as daughter and sister was no longer a sturdy fit. I was a traditional girl. I planned on being married for life.

We were married, we *are* married—this is what we pledged to each other that October afternoon when he slipped the ring onto my finger, me all sweaty under my dress and fully riled up on nerves and excitement, when he looked right at me and said "I do."

But now one of us was moving into a new apartment and getting his creativity back.

Whatever the hell that means.

Charlie needed to get his creativity back, and I was a barrier to that goal. I heard him, but it still seemed negotiable, hadn't sunk in.

"Please," I begged him one night. "Just tell me if you've met someone else." I knew he had. I'd heard the whispered late-night phone calls downstairs while he thought I was in bed asleep. I knew it . . . but I wanted him to *say* it.

"I just think we need this time apart . . . ," he said.

Why do men always think it's easier to tell a woman that he left her sorry self because something was missing, instead of saying he'd found someone new? We can handle being passed over for something prettier. Well. All right, *perhaps* we won't handle it gracefully at the get-go, but it is at least a scenario we can logically parse out—feel like we somehow aren't the sole reason for their leaving. But telling a woman you left her just because you'd be happier alone than by her side? It's not a kindness. I wanted him to tell me the truth, tell me a name, tell me he'd fallen out of love, something. Anything.

That night I came home and the living room was the exact same, except for the huge void where the sofa had been. I opened the hall closet and lost my breath when I saw he'd even taken his winter coats, old Rollerblades, faded tennis balls. He wasn't fooling around with the leaving part.

I walked up the four beige bi-level stairs into his office. It was a wide room, at least ten or twelve feet, with cold linoleum on the floor that echoed with each footstep. Frankie the cat was in the corner sitting sentry.

Frankie had always been his cat. We had two felines at the beginning of our marriage, both adopted from a local shelter about a week after we got married. Those animals had been our sole companions until the morning of my birthday a few years back when Charlie had discovered two flea-bitten scrawny kittens behind the garage. We'd taken them to the vet ("Please, take them!"), but the vet was full ("No room at the inn"), and of course by the end of the evening we'd named them: Frankie and Bob.

You name something and it's yours; that's a fact.

Having four cats didn't seem so god-awful weird when it was the two of us living in a good-sized condo, so we weren't at all crowded. And little Frankie, a round-faced female calico with giant white whiskers, adored my husband Charlie. She sat at his feet each night as he typed away at his computer, or lined her whole body up along the back of his office chair, stretched out and content. The cats had just become part of our goofy life together, something we made jokes about, and at night they slept at the foot of the bed or in the basket on the windowsill. We were a family, albeit one with twenty legs between us all.

I looked at Frankie. Ten hours earlier, this empty room had been full of his bookshelves, books, CDs, posters, a rug from IKEA—all of it gone. I cried like something had come unhinged inside me. Frankie sat in a corner and mewed like she was wounded, and we echoed, me with big strings of snot and tears all down my shirt, Frankie with her animal knowledge that everything was wrong and changed.

That was where I spent the first night without him.

Too afraid to go upstairs to the bedroom and see his side of the closet cleaned of his hanging clothes and shoes, unable to face an empty bathroom cabinet or to smell him on the pillows, too tired and used up to even take off my shoes, I sat there with the cat that had loved him so purely. I slid down onto the linoleum floor and cried, and later, when I wanted to cry but couldn't, I stared at the walls. Toward dawn, I washed my face in the kitchen sink and put on lipstick, and when the sun came up, I went into work in the same clothes I'd worn the day before.

He was gone.

Chapter 4

· ·

Between Charlie's moving out and my eventual resettling into my own place, I was in limbo, suspended between my old life and what would become my new post-him life. The three months that followed can pretty much be summed up as easy as a math problem: If a woman, traveling at too many miles per hour toward her unforeseeable future, can drink X amounts of red wine out of a chipped coffee cup, will it be Patsy Cline or George Jones on the stereo at midnight?

There were furious hurricanes in Florida that year, and I watched the news obsessively all night, calling my folks and waking them from their bed on the west Florida coast, asking them if they felt the outer bands of the storm yet. They listened patiently as I described in great detail what the weather forecasters in Biloxi or Lake Charles or Tampa were saying, broadcast into my TV set thanks to the modern marvel of twenty-four-hour news channels.

During those nights, I was about as close to feeling anything outside myself as I could get. I was consumed with the hurricanes, and I'm sure my coworkers enjoyed the way I talked about barometric pressure as if it were my health.

People must have smelled the stink of heartbreak on me and given me a wide space to move in, completely fogged up with loneliness and sorrow, and hungover like nobody's business.

Aside from wind velocity and millibars of atmospheric pressure happening in states eleven hundred miles away, what I was doing on any given day or wearing or surviving is a mystery, maybe locked away forever so I don't have to relive what can surely be the worst fashion choices and worst behavior of my life.

I can remember in stark detail, however, what it felt like to wake up one morning out on the patio, shivering in an old wooden Adirondack chair, because I was too afraid to sleep inside the place he and I used to call home. I looked down at my sock feet and missed the way I used to rest my feet on his long legs, how I could put my face up to the back of his neck while he was still asleep in the mornings and a cat would lie at the foot of the bed or next to me, and we were all one warm blanket of breathing.

During that time, I moved numbly from one foul mix-up to the next, each new turn of bad luck just something I ciphered into my ledger of failure. My car got stolen from the subway parking lot on the day of our wedding anniversary. Then Charlie went to Italy without me; was a girlfriend keeping him warm? Los Angeles erupted in the worst fire season in a decade, and I sat out on the patio each night under the burned black-orange sky, smoking even though the air was so thick with ash it was redundant. Just inhale. The owner of our beloved condo sent me a registered letter that he was selling the property, and I had a few weeks to find a new place to live. The hurricanes kept coming, and I was simply immovable, stuck, nothing but pressure building in poor atmospheric conditions, drinking whatever came with a warning label.

My friend Jennifer would come over and sit on the floor with me as I chain-smoked the three thousandth cigarette and played the same country song over, and over, and over, puddled up in a corner, believing that at any moment I would probably die of some weird broken-heart-related illness that involved visible panty lines and grief and acne.

I do not believe it was a stretch of the imagination to say I smelled bad. Disheveled, rumpled, covered in cat hair, and my house was a mess. She listened to me cry and refilled my drink and never, ever once said an unkind word about me or a nice one about Charlie.

Now that is a very good friend.

Jennifer and I had met at work some years back and we just clicked. I didn't even mind that she was as skinny as my whole left thigh. I loved her all the way through, and she somehow managed to stay by my side through every day of "the crazy time." And the "Oh My God You Played George Jones For Seven Hours Straight" time.

The decorum I had carefully developed through years of training began to falter. I'd smile one minute, and the next, I'd break apart into a slobbering heap. That is what the failure of a marriage does to you: It breaks you right at your heart and travels through your whole body so you feel public-faced and "together" half the time, and the other half you spend flying into places unknown even to yourself, a kind of unspeakable despair and anger and finally, cold resentment that scares your family and makes them show up for a visit at Thanksgiving even though your dad hates cats and your brother goes into an asthmatic fit at the sight of one, and you yourself are covered in cat hair from the knees down, and your mother hugs you just the same, and you drive from the airport to your condo and talk about traffic and weather and their flight like everything was right as rain on Sunday.

Chapter 5

· ·

When my parents arrived in Los Angeles, I was about a minute and a half from directing traffic in my nightgown, talking into my bra, and covering the windows with tinfoil.

They sensed this the way parents sense you've been secretly smoking cigarettes in tenth grade, and they flew out with my baby brother Eric to make sure I kept the tinfoil securely housed in the kitchen drawer. And also because they love me, and I am their only daughter, and I had been quoting country songs to them over the phone.

They stayed for an entire week. My parents took the morning paper and circled some apartments in the want ads and we drove around and visited one apartment—just one—and later I cried in the car so quietly and completely that they never said a word about it. There is nothing as incongruent in this world as being a married thirty-three-year-old woman sniveling in the backseat of your parents' rented car as they try to help you find a shitty one-bedroom apartment that takes cats. But I knew of course that I had to move; the lease on the condo was up soon, and I had to find someplace to live.

Charlie had all but disappeared by then.

We no longer talked on the phone, and he lived more in my mind and the pictures I had of the two of us than in my day-to-day life. I guess I knew somewhere deep inside that it was over the day he walked out the door, but I'd hung in a state of suspended gloom for months until my folks showed up with the classified ads and bags of groceries and a full bottle of single-malt Scotch.

One evening in the middle of their visit (my wheezing brother having long gone to stay with a catless friend), we were making dinner—Dad was cooking the main dish, while my mom and I were making fresh cocktails and simmering a white wine–butter sauce with artichoke hearts and capers and sundried tomatoes. My mom told me to add the lemon juice, and I dumped in the equivalent of thirty-seven acres of fresh lemons. We tasted the sauce and puckered up and spit it out over the sink. Later we conspired to blame this sauce misfortune on my dad, and he took it good-naturedly the way only a dad can do when his child is coming unglued and he's here to put her back together. We ended up having the best dinner that night: barbecued halibut and green beans and rice and the sauce that made your mouth go inside out from the tartness.

"Daddy," I said. "I'm sorry."

"For what?" he said. "The sauce is perfect."

And we just looked at each other. He patted my leg, then reached out and gave me a full hug—the force of it unexpected.

In his own tacit way, he was saying he'd seen morose before. I wasn't anything he couldn't handle. There was a comfort in that moment that somehow anchored me, brought me back to reality long enough to think I might, just maybe, make it out of this thing.

Chapter 6

. . . .

My parents flew back to Florida, and on a rainy day in December I looked at my calendar and realized I had two weeks to find a new home for me, four cats, twenty-seven pairs of shoes, and my insomnia. It appeared that The Last Minute had officially arrived.

I'd like to tell you I put nose to the grindstone and set about this task like an adult. Truth is, I took the first place I looked at. I walked into the tiny 800-square-foot house, and it was raining so hard that the property owner couldn't show me the yard or the garage, but I filled out my credit application anyway. I'll never know why he took a chance on me that night, especially after I explained to him I had no real credit history (all of that was in Charlie's name)—maybe I looked so mournful and bedraggled that the man saw something in me that needed kindness. He said he could let me move in on the twentieth. Five days before Christmas.

There was relief, for a moment. Then dread. I procrastinated with the packing as if magic grief gnomes would rise from the cool, white interior of our married life and cart me off into some cloudy future unseen. I couldn't even remember what the inside of my newly rented house looked like. I forgot to call the gas company. I ran out of boxes. I cried each time I found something that reminded me of him, us; I smashed three picture frames and barbecued a stack of Polaroids in the Weber charcoal grill on the patio.

I was perhaps not exactly ready for this new life transition.

When the movers arrived I could see their surprise at all the mess and disorder, and I didn't even care. "My husband left me," I told the one who spoke English.

By this time I had become so wholly unhinged that I no longer filtered the sad details from an unsuspecting public, just from coworkers and distant family. He translated my despair into Spanish for his co-movers, and they hauled all that crap into boxes, taped them up, and put them on the truck.

Nine hours later my stuff was in a tiny house on the far fringes of Los Angeles, a house now packed floor to ceiling with all the years of my marital effort. I sat out on the patio, on one of eight green plastic tubs full of handpicked Christmas decorations, smoking cigarettes and feeling like a person who's about to be swallowed up whole by despair. I looked at my checkbook, now nine hundred dollars lighter, looked at the mountains of boxes, looked at my grimy clothes, and bawled.

Chapter 7

* *

"I should probably unpack."

I walked around the house, maneuvering between piles of boxes, and repeating it as a mantra. Over and over. *I should probably unpack.*

Of the expansive 811 square feet of my newly rented house, the most enjoyable feature was . . . the outside of it. Specifically, the patio region where I sat each night and drank wine and smoked cigarettes because it was scary indoors what with the now-missing husband and the seven thousand boxes of our failed marriage and the cats, and, apparently, a new drinking problem.

Oh, and let us not forget about the boxes.

When Charlie moved out, he took exactly what he wanted from our Married Life and left the rest of the years of collected, assorted junk and stuff for me to deal with. At first I assumed this was because we'd be getting back together at any moment, but it didn't take long to realize that he had maybe moved on, and I was here under threat of imminent death because of the Box Situation. Who knew when the Jaws of Life would be called upon to wrench me out from under a large pile of mismatched kitchenware, piles of blankets, and eight hundred assorted knickknacks?

My friend Shannon called every few days to check in on me and make sure I hadn't been trapped under a mountain of clutter and grief. Shannon is a redheaded fireball, a tiny pale-skinned beauty who has known me since I was still young enough to pass for nineteen. She knew Charlie. Right after he moved out, she would come over to visit and bring her big tapestry knitting bag and sit on the floor and listen to me bellyache and carry on and drink dark, foul-smelling drinks from a coffee cup.

One night I watched her carefully pull yarn around a needle, making a fluffy mohair scarf. (I learned later that I have a genetic attraction to mohair, and it conceals cat hair well.)

"Shannon," I asked. "Are you *knitting*?"

"I am indeed," she said. "Knitting is the new yoga. You should take up knitting, Laurie! It would be good for you. Everyone does it on the sets of movies. Even Julia Roberts knits."

Shannon is an actress in Los Angeles. I worked at a bank and had a broken heart, visible panty lines, and a cracked coffee cup welded to my hand.

"I don't do yoga."

Shannon had learned to knit at Lani's Needlepoint, a local yarn shop on Ventura Boulevard in Studio City. "It's very chic," she told me. "You just show up for the class, pay a fee, and they help you pick out yarn and needles, and then they show you all the basic stuff so you can make a scarf." She was on her eleventy-ninth scarf.

When she first asked me to go with her and learn to knit just like Julia Roberts, I was still very early in the Batshit Crazy process. Even the most simple activities had become impossible. I'd be at the store buying wine and cat food, and I'd see someone with *his* favorite brand of cereal and I'd burst into sniffling, poorly concealed tears.

Maybe Shannon was right, after all. Maybe I needed a hobby.

I looked around at my house. Just a pile of stuff, half in and half out of boxes, shoes in a mountain by the front door. I was a thirty-something woman living alone with four cats. I was probably going to be divorced. I was on the short bus to crazy. I pictured my grandmother making hoopskirted yarn cozies for the toilet paper. I pictured myself making doilies for furniture that I did not own. I saw my cats wearing knitted hats with lace appliqués. From my vantage point, knitting seemed like 100 percent of some road I did not want to walk down.

"I need a freshen-up on my coffee cup," I said to Shannon. Changing the subject. "Can I get you anything?"

No, I was just sure that knitting was not for me.

But Shannon hadn't given up on inviting me to her class. In fact, once I had developed insomnia and a new, hermitlike attitude, she began to mention it more and more. She would show me her creations, long, silky shawls and soft, nubby, skinny scarves with fringe or ribbons at the end.

On a rainy Saturday in January, I walked into the kitchen of my little clutter box of a new house to make a cup of (unadulterated) real coffee. I tried to find the coffee pot in a labyrinth of cardboard and bubble wrap and after fifteen minutes of contemplating the storage unit known as My Kitchen, I called Shannon.

"Where is this knitting class, exactly?"
You could feel the smile on the other end of the phone.
Shannon and New Yoga: One
Laurie the Spinster: Zero.

Chapter 8

. . . .

The yarn shop was nothing I remembered from the shopping excursions with my grandmother to the Woolworths in Corpus Christi, Texas. I used to wander the aisles looking for treasures (clackers were my favorite—how we did not all end up maimed after growing up in the South in the '70s and whacking each other hard with clackers is a mystery still unsolved to this very day), and my grandma, who we all called Oma, would pick out a few skeins of acrylic yarn from open bins near the sewing supplies and spend long, intense moments gazing at the fancy silver scissors.

Oma crocheted. She made itchy and fabulously ugly slippers for us kids each Christmas, which we wore all morning until some horrible tragedy befell them (dogs were always great coconspirators in the effort, as were sticky substances, snags in the floorboards, and when desperate, nail clippers). Oma's yarn colors were a 1976 rainbow of orange, dark orange, yellow, pale yellow, brown, and sometimes a deep maroon. The yarn selection in Woolworths looked like deconstructed candy corn.

I expected to see the same selection at the Studio City store, with perhaps a nice teal or green thrown into the mix. But as soon as I opened the door to the yarn shop, I realized we were not in my grandmother's Woolworths. There were baskets piled high with thick, lush wool; crinkled ribbons; silk yarn as fine as thread—everything rich and soft—and even a huge bin of sparkly, wispy yarns I had never seen before.

"Is this *yarn*?" I asked the sales clerk.

"Yes, it's called eyelash yarn," she said. "It's very soft, and lots of people use it for scarves."

I walked around for twenty minutes with instructions to select a simple yarn, nothing too wispy or chunky, because apparently it's easier to learn this New Yoga on a simple yarn. I finally picked out a soft wool in deep multicolored strands with a tiny ladder of deep gold thread mixed in. It was luscious. *And expensive.* The ninety-nine-cent yarn of my youth had been replaced in the past few decades with what can only be described as *Ohmygod I am paying twelve dollars for this?*

The knitting shop had a wide selection of needles, too. I sort of had my heart set on the spinster needles of my nightmare, thin wooden sticks with little balls on the end—just like every granny-in-a-rocking-chair postcard you've seen at Cracker Barrel. But the shop clerk selected a pair of fine ebony Lantern Moon wooden needles in a size appropriate for my chosen yarn. Purchases in hand, I had no excuses left, so I walked toward the table in the back of the store, a long, sturdy wood table with a handful of women seated around it in varying stages of knitting. I joined them, and the knitting teacher introduced herself, and after a few minutes I learned to cast on and how to hold the needles. Then she demonstrated the knit stitch.

I have always been an overachiever. Not at sports of course, because after all, I am built for comfort, not speed. But at anything requiring manual dexterity or brain power, I am a bona fide nerd and desperate know-it-all. I assumed that if generations of women in caves and thatch huts could learn to knit, so could I with my overfed brain and deep love of television. But it took me a while to get the motions just right. I struggled at first, wanting my knit stitches to be perfect. I perhaps held the yarn in a death grip, as if my personal issues were taking a toll on one pretty, but not terribly soothing, ball of yarn.

"Dear," said the knitting teacher. "You may want to loosen up your grip on the yarn."

"It might divorce me if I let it get away," I said. Shannon shot me a sideways glance. The teacher, blessedly, said nothing.

After about ten minutes, it clicked. Something inside the recesses of my sleep-deprived brain *got the knit stitch.*

"I am doing the knit stitch," I announced, proudly, to no one in particular.

"That's awesome!" People in yarn shops are very encouraging, even when the class consists of four nice people and one crazy Crackerass McCracker and her friend Shannon.

"It's also called the garter stitch," said the teacher. "You're doing it just perfect!"

I bought another ball of yarn on my way out of the shop, said goodbye to Shannon, and went home. I should have walked into my house full of accomplishment and resolve. I should have finally found the gusto to unpack, to face my lot in life, messy and chaotic as it might be. I should have possibly vacuumed.

Instead, I walked in the front door, placed my keys on the temporary side table (three cardboard boxes and a stack of newspapers), and sat on the sofa with my new activity. I knitted. And I knitted. The cats sniffed the yarn, batted at the needles, and after this exertion left them exhausted, slept in various piles of clothes and packing material. I knitted as if my very sanity depended on creating a scarf worthy of Julia Roberts herself.

Chapter 9

· ·

My parents called me on Sunday to "check in," which is code for See If She's Gone Off The Deep End Yet.

"I'm knitting!" I told my mom. "I have completed at least one quarter of a real scarf! I wasn't sure what to do when I got to the very end of my first ball of yarn, because, well, I just learned this yesterday. But I double-stranded and knit on like a madwoman. It's the New Yoga!"

"You never did the old yoga," said my mother. Lovingly, I assume.

"Yes, but this is better because I can sit on the sofa without any painful pretzel poses and drink wine while doing the New Yoga, which to my knowledge is the primary downfall of the Old Yoga—no wine."

"Have you slept?" she asked.

"Are you kidding?" I said. "No. But it isn't because of the whole Oh My God I Am Spurned thing! I am knitting!"

"Well," she said. Slowly. Picking through just the right words, as I was prone to spontaneous tears brought on by even the kindest sentiments. "I'm glad you have a new hobby. But don't you think you should try to get some sleep? Maybe see your doctor about a light sleeping aid?"

"I'm going to knit all my Christmas presents this year! And birthday gifts. And *Mother's Day* gifts! It will be fabulous."

The other end of the line was studiously silent.

"Don't worry," I said. "It won't be little candy corn–colored slippers. Promise. Bye! I have to go knit some more!"

———

*I*n her defense, my mom was probably not swooning with happiness over my newfound obsession with knitting (and in particular, making all future gifts, gifts with love! Gifts from the heart!). My mom has endured years, I mean *years* of homemade crap from me, her artistic if rather demented child. So with my new knitting obsession she was likely worried that I was going to make her a gift, full of *love* and also *ugliness*, that she'd have to wear forever and secretly hate me for giving her on Mother's Day, a holiday meant to honor her, not torture her.

I spent the greater part of my formative years making my parents "artsy" stuff like:

- Ages 3–5: Macaroni-encrusted pencil holders, macaroni collages, macaroni anything. (It was the '70s.)

- Ages 6–7: Lumpy ashtrays for my family of *nonsmokers*.

- Age 8: One nature collage made of poison ivy, poison oak, and sumac. Boy, was that one a hit, especially when I was lying in a calamine lotion bath all summer.

- Ages 9–13: Random 4-H camp creations, aka "the lanyard years."

- Ages 13–17: Paintings of teenage angst.

- Age 18–present: Things I refer to as "kitschy" to mask their awfulness.

I'm sure she was waiting with bated breath for my newest creation, which she *would be obligated to wear* every time she saw me until her 100 percent wool scarf or shawl or mittens got mysteriously eaten by giant Florida moths or swept away by a freak Homemade Crap Vortex (HCV).

My mom has a warped sense of humor. During the stay-at-home-mom years, she maybe, just maybe, had a small child who was a total living terror who, until he was about age six, cried every two and a half minutes. And this same mom, stressed out with two teenagers and a baby and also kind of pissed that the universe gave her a rotten kid, decided that one day she would maybe cook a hamburger in the shape of a hot dog, and serve the hamburger in a hot-dog bun, just to *freak out* her four-year-old. And then she told the story repeatedly about how he finally stopped crying because he was so puzzled and entranced with her hot-burger creation.

Placed in the context of my family, I make so much more sense. I knew my mom was wondering what sort of creation I would knit that would cover her toilet paper with yarn and glitter and if it would be in the shape of a cat.

Chapter 10

All I had heard since Charlie moved out was, "Laurie, maybe you should take up a hobby or something. Stay busy, it will keep your mind off things." Har har. Well, the joke's on you now, all you future recipients of thousands of scarves! I have a hobby, dammit!

I loved knitting so much that I didn't even care how well it cemented my role as the crazy cat lady spinster. At work, I proudly showed off my knitting to every single person who stopped by my desk. You want a banner ad? First, admire my knitting! You need a logo resized? No problem, let me tell you all about knitting class!

I knitted at night. I knitted during my commute time on the bus. Must finish. Must do just one more row. Must count stitches—whoops, twenty-one? Could have sworn I began with twenty. Oh well, I'll just knit those two together. Voilà. Now must keep knitting. Must. Not. Stop.

I learned how to bind off a scarf and cast on for another one. I learned how to add yarn so that it didn't ripple across a row (double-stranding was not, apparently, the best method for adding yarn). I carefully selected new needles, larger ones for airier projects, smaller needles for smaller yarn. I knitted scarf after scarf, and eventually I let go of my standards of perfection, happy to have another completed project (and another new one to start!).

When I finally decided to break free of the rectangle, I learned to knit hats, and because I have problems following even the most basic of patterns, I started making my own (with sometimes disastrously hilarious results). Knitting filled long hours at night, long hours on the bus to and from work, lunch hours when I was incapable of socializing in the break room.

It became a quiet place, controlled. If something wasn't working out, you didn't have to just abandon it, give up on all the time you'd spent with it, get your creativity back somewhere else . . . you could rip out the stitches and start all over again, from the beginning. No matter what the mistake, you could always go back and make it better. It was very reassuring.

Part 2
Unraveling

Chapter 11

Things that mattered back then seem ridiculous now.

That time we argued about where to eat dinner. Someone waits too long at the train station, someone doesn't remember to buy . . . ? I don't remember now. What was it I forgot to buy?

Was I demanding?

What is demanding?

Is it wrong to demand love, truth, the first kiss of the day, a hand on the small of your back when you're in a crowd? A husband to care for you and bring you a magazine because he knew you liked the movie star on the cover? I am sitting on my patio, and it is raining, and I'm afraid to bring my knitting outside because a moth the size of a small-occupancy aircraft is perched on the back of a patio chair. The moths must sense that I have been hoarding yarn, a lovely Lopi wool in muted earth tones.

So I'm just thinking, with a glass of wine. Again.

I try to picture the two of us sitting back at our old place. I don't know why I do this to myself—it's like slow death.

"What would you say if I told you I wanted to have a baby?"

In my memory, it is winter, I'm in front of the fireplace petting a cat, and Charlie is on the sofa, randomly flipping through channels on the television set. Apparently nothing can hold his interest. Or maybe he hasn't found what he is looking for?

"What would you say if I told you I wanted to have a baby?" I ask.

I had decided that our problems, our isolation, the loneliness I felt inside could be solved if we just had a baby. After all, the logical move after you go to school and get a job is to Get Married, and the logical step after that is Have A Family, and even though I wasn't sure I wanted a baby, I wasn't sure we were ready, I was grasping, holding on, trying in the only ways I knew how to bring us back together. I wanted closeness. I wanted love.

"What would you say if I told you I wanted to have a baby?" I ask.

"Oh," he says. As if I were asking the question of the cat or maybe the TV.

He pauses. But I am tireless, I never stop, do I? So I ask again, because this time, this time his shrug, his selective deafness, his "I don't hear you" will not satisfy me.

"What would you say if I told you I wanted to have a baby?"

"I'd say we need to travel more, because we'd be stuck here after a baby."

I had my answer.

Chapter 12

· ·

When someone has been a part of your daily life for so long, the loss of him creates a void that feels almost unfillable, especially at first. I wonder if other women going through a divorce take up some new hobby they never imagined themselves doing? Do they become stamp collectors? Or another woman, perhaps one with less vices, does she take up running? Bowling? Snowshoeing in a cold climate?

Do some women start dating from the outset, meet a new man, fill the empty place? I cannot even imagine that. It seems like a foreign film from another planet.

When Charlie moved out, I moved *way in.* After a while, I didn't leave my house. *Ever.* Aside from going to work and going to the 7-Eleven for groceries, which is where all normal people shop for groceries, I just channeled Howard Hughes and envisioned the impermeable bubble of my dreams. My friends would invite me out to have brunch, go shopping. I wanted to go—I really did—but I was so terrified, so sad, so isolated that I stayed home, watched TV, and sat on the floor with a bottle of wine. And oh, by the way, drinking alone? Totally one of those symptoms mentioned on the AA checklist. Drinking alone while watching reruns of *Growing Pains* and talking to your cat about love gone wrong? *Totally embarrassing.*

This type of living is what I call my "Fear Life."

In my Fear Life, I would ideally work from home, submitting my projects remotely and never attending meetings or going to an office. I would piddle in my garden and knit and talk to my cats, and before long groceries would get delivered (not shopped for, even at 7-Eleven), catalogs would replace the mall, and friends would come visit but only if they followed The Golden Hermit Rule: Call before you come over, e-mail before you call, and think twice before you e-mail.

In time, in the Fear Life, days become so insulated and alone that even things I love to do—like travel—would be too scary and I would eventually miss out on my own life. For some people, the Fear Life takes on a different bent (partying too much, wild, sleepless nights on the town), but for me, the Fear Life is total seclusion, an extra forty pounds, and avoiding eye contact.

My friends would come to my house and visit with me, but aside from that I had become closed up inside myself somehow, locked out of normal socialization either by my choice or my sadness. Maybe both. Going to that knitting class was a risk. Talking to strangers, hoping they didn't ask too many personal questions, it was just pure terror.

But I needed to do it.

It seems like such a small thing, leaving your house and knitting with a small group of people who also like yarn. But my emotions were unpredictable at best, and I often chose to stay inside, way down inside. I wished there had been a handbook for it. A friend gave me the name of an old self-help book from the 1970s that had helped him through a rough patch, and so I bought it that very same day, hoping it would be the divorce how-to guide perfectly tailored for me. I read it all night, cover to cover. I'm sure it might have helped some people, but I was wondering where the chapter was on burying the bodies.

So I knitted some more, entranced at the magical way knits and purls lined up perfectly even when everything else around me went awry.

Chapter 13

· ·

Strangely enough, it was knitting that rescued me from isolating myself and from becoming the crazy cat lady of my nightmares.

Had I taken up stamp collecting or pottery or cross-country unicycling, I am sure I would have met equally interesting and happy people who shared my love of the newfound activity.

But I had picked up sticks and string, so it was through knitting that my new life took a rather unexpected turn for the better. That very first knitting class with Shannon had gone so well that I attended another, and yet another.

I had started purchasing knitting books as if they were going out of print and reading patterns at night when I couldn't sleep. Seeing the glossy photos of items way above my own skill level or ambition made me happy and kept my mind occupied with complex stitch patterns. Thoughts of soon-to-be-ex-husbands, holidays alone, and childless, lonely years—they all dimmed in the face of a lace inset or carefully constructed mitten.

Then Annie Modesitt came to town.

Annie was a well-known, famous knitter with a line of published books and patterns. She was most famous at that time for her unique method of knitting and a special way of making cable patterns.

She was going to be teaching a series of knitting classes at Unwind, a local yarn shop in the Valley. Even though my urge to stay indoors and lock myself away with my sadness and a sturdy cabernet was quite strong, my desire to learn about new knitting techniques was stronger.

It really wasn't such bad advice, after all, people telling me to get a hobby.

I signed up for the class, and for weeks I talked about my upcoming "Cabling without a Cable Needle" knitting seminar to all my friends, whose eyes glazed over with a look of painful boredom. I tried to explain to my non-knitting friends that Annie Modesitt was a real, bona fide knitting legend. It's as if you were taking guitar lessons from Jimi Hendrix, only with less LSD and pot-smoking.

On the day of the class, I woke up about seventeen hours early and struggled with what to wear. I'd kind of lost my interest in looking presentable, but I wanted to look not homeless or crazy. Then I fretted over which needles and yarn to take, finally stuffing twelve different pairs of knitting needles in my bag.

I arrived late, 100 percent nervous, and sweaty. I had grown unaccustomed to making small talk with strangers and hoped no one would try to speak to me. I worried, praying I could cast on and knit and purl well enough to follow the class and not make a complete idiot of myself. I hoped I didn't puddle up into a mess if someone was knitting a fabulous sweater for a faithful and supportive husband or a pair of booties for a perfect child. I hoped

I didn't talk about my husbandless, childless self. I hoped I would not talk about my cats as if they were people.

Annie was lovely and animated, and she made everyone at the table feel welcomed.

And the other people in the class were so nice. Everyone just chatted and cabled and helped each other out. Well, there might have been this one woman who was not so much into it. When I arrived I took the only remaining seat at the table (at the left hand of Annie, the weight and portent of which were not lost on me), and the woman seated to *my* left . . . well, she just up and left five minutes into the class. Apparently being seated at the left hand of Crazy Old Cat Lady is not quite the same religious experience. I'm not one to be paranoid, much, but I did wonder if I had somehow been the reason she left. When she found out I was Southern did she immediately have the urge to flee? Was it something I said? Was it when I tried to convince the tableful of Californians that Texas was an alright place because of sweet tea? Maybe she was on one of those low-carb diets and the mere mention of sweet tea sent her on a bender? It was so weird. She just stood up and walked out.

I was thrown off for a moment, but after her mysterious disappearing act, class became very entertaining. Especially when we all tried to read from a chart. And do yarn overs. Somehow I got tricked into using teeny, small-sized needles, but I was so nervous to do a good job for Annie, goddess of knitting, that I did not even complain.

She had a keen observation about knitting mistakes—she told the class that messing up is actually a *good* thing, a desirable thing, so you can learn from your errors. I was a superb student, too, since messing up is my specialty (see: whole life, especially four cats, divorce, one potty mouth, wine lips).

I loved her passion for her work and her sense of humor. And let's face it, a sense of humor is critical in knitting, especially my knitting ("Oh, I'll be damned, I'm knitting this whole thing inside out. Isn't that funny!"). Sometimes knitting books and tutorials can be a bit dense. There's a lot of very technical detail in knitting, which I can definitely appreciate, but to me the whole joy of making fabric from string and chopsticks is the sheer surprise of seeing it all come together, a handmade wonder, knots and all.

With her sense of humor, Annie was speaking a language I could get. Because if you listen to me knit—and I do knit out loud—it's so, so charming, for the first five seconds, and then you want to kill me—anyway, after listening to me struggle with a pattern, you will eventually begin to think that "Shit!" is a type of knit stitch. As in, "Okay, here I knit one, purl two, yarn over, Shit! Knit two more. . . ." Not that Annie Modesitt said the s-word, of course. She is a trained professional. Even though I may have accidentally done my knit-out-loud thing once or twice in class, no one so much as shot me a mean glance. And Annie was such an amazing knitter—lightning fast and witty and kind—and even though she likely suspected I was a total stalker ("Hi! I read your book cover to cover so many times! Hi! I love your website!"), she never even tried to call the law once.

After three hours and a few successful cable swatches, I left class, drove home, and felt as if I had conquered something. I was so proud of myself. I called my parents and told them all about my weekend and my class.

My dad was so happy for me, and that was when I heard it in his voice. Relief. It surprised me a little because I hadn't realized my parents were so worried about my sanity. But they'd seen me change and hole up in my house for almost six months, and my cheerful calls to them usually consisted of *some funny thing my cat did,* which scares a parent, y'all know. They lived far away and couldn't draw me out of my shell, and I could hear how happy they were for me to meet new people and go out and live life.

Plus, it's way easier to explain to friends that your child in Los Angeles is just going through a tough patch but has taken up knitting, than to admit she's gone buckwild crazy and is wearing her bra on her head and directing traffic on Sixth and Main. They were relieved.

Chapter 14

Emboldened by my excellent class experience, and through the magic of the Internet ("There are pedophiles on the Internet," warned my mother. "I saw a special on *Dateline*."), I discovered other knitters as well. Some had websites and others used the Internet to post the times and dates of their weekly meetings. I was intrigued, a group of completely unrelated strangers meeting on a regular day and knitting together? I absolutely adored the name: Stitch 'n Bitch. There was even a book by the same name, and a sequel, both of which I bought immediately upon learning of their existence.

I was insanely curious about Stitching 'n Bitching. Was it awkward? Were the women nice? (I assumed it was all women, an assumption that later proved to be false.) Were they older women? Or the young Hollywood starlet types? Did it matter? They were knitters, after all, and I was desperate to have more people to share my interest in my newfound obsessive hobby. I had long since bored all my coworkers with rhapsodies about 100 percent hand-dyed wool yarn and Addi Turbo knitting needles.

It was Ellen Bloom that changed everything. A complete stranger to me, Ellen was one of the key members at the West

Hollywood Stitch 'n Bitch group. She had seen my own little knitting website, a hasty affair I'd thrown together when I was stuck with insomnia and no one at all to talk to, and she e-mailed me a single, perfect note:

Dear Laurie,

Why don't you come join us at the West Hollywood Stitch 'n Bitch? We'd love to meet you and might even teach you to crochet.

Yours, Ellen Bloom

I forwarded that e-mail immediately to Jennifer and called her on the phone before she had the time to respond.

"I want to go to this Stitching Bitching thing. Did you get the e-mail I just sent you?"

"Please do not tell me you just called to see if I had received an e-mail," she said. This is a joke with us, since my parents were rather well known for calling me to see if I had gotten their e-mails, as if technology were so unruly one had to check up on it at every corner.

"I want to go, but . . . ," I trailed off. "What if they hate me?"

"Why would they hate you?" said Jennifer.

"Because I talk too much when I get nervous, and sometimes I cry," I said. "This is not exactly a newsflash to you."

"I'm sure they'll like you," said Jennifer. "You really are insane, you know."

"How is it that those two sentences, said side by side, do not reassure me?"

I knew I must attend this fabled Stitch 'n Bitch, even if just to satisfy my curiosity on what the general population of modern-day knitters looked like. My main issue was that I had become quite reclusive by then, and I refused to go by myself. I was terrified of meeting new people, peeling back my carefully constructed hiding place, venturing out and meeting folks, even if they were knitters, introducing myself to strangers when I wasn't sure myself of who I was now. It always came back to that, didn't it? Who was I, anymore?

Shannon, my knitting enabler, was busy with a live theater show in North Hollywood, and she rehearsed on Thursdays. Obviously the knitting group met on Thursdays, because that is my luck. Jennifer had recently started her first year of law school and she was overwhelmed with reading and assignments, and a good friend, indeed a *best* friend, would never have insisted she give up a full evening of studying for a fancy law degree just to go knitting with some strangers at a food court in West Hollywood.

I made Jennifer go with me. I might have even warbled a bit on the phone, and gained sympathy. I *really* wanted to meet these knitting people.

We arrived precisely on time and nervously weaved our way through the West Hollywood Farmer's Market. According to Ellen, the group met at the upstairs eating area, where there were wide tables and plenty of room to spread out.

I was terrified.

I tried to back out four times in four minutes.

Jennifer took me by the arm, and for a little thing she really has some surprising upper-body strength. She propelled me forward, and we walked up the stairs together, knitting bags at the ready. Jen had unearthed a half-finished scarf from her first attempt to knit a few years back, and I was armed with three scarves and a hat. At the top of the stairway, we looked around like little turtles, tentatively peeking at the crowd until we spotted about five women circling a table, yarn and magazines spread out between them.

They saw us, bobbing and weaving through the tables, and welcomed us straightaway. All that built-up terror and fear just melted away with a big welcoming hug from one Ellen Bloom in the flesh.

"Hi there!" She was friendly and seemed happy to have both Jennifer and me there for a Thursday night knit-along. She introduced me to some of the other ladies at the table, and then pointed out a lovely woman with a soft pageboy haircut. "And this is Audrey; she's the one who found your website to begin with," said Ellen. And I got a hug from Audrey, too, and we all sat down, and I felt welcomed, and my paralyzing shyness and fear began to drain out little by little.

All this time I had been living in Los Angeles and wondering where all the *real* people were. Apparently they were knitting! I had no idea. Not that I don't love this city—I do—but it's so hard to meet folks here who aren't hard and bright like so many little twinkling plastic jewels, teetering on high-high heels, drinking anything with "-*tini*" on the end, and being fabulous, which I find exhausting. I am not always fabulous.

But the women (and one man!) we met that night were smart and funny and diverse and welcoming and lovely, and all I can tell you is that at some point we began a critical analysis of cheeseburger offerings in the greater Los Angeles metropolitan region, and that made me feel like I was finally, at last, At Home.

Meeting new people is really nerve-racking for me. I say incredibly inappropriate things, and when I get nervous I manage to blurt out nonsense, so it was a big night for me, Spinster Hermit Lady, on many levels.

1) I actually left my house, at night.

2) I actually left the Valley.

3) *I met strangers.*

4) I got to knit with people who thought I was a knitter! Note to self: My strategy for using knits and purls to seem like a more advanced knitter than I am is working like a charm.

5) I didn't cry.

6) I only used one swear word. Or maybe two.

7) Jennifer and I got to knit together for the first time *ever.*

8) Jen appeared to like knitting, which made me incredibly happy, like we'd both up and joined the Moonies, but in a good way.

9) I managed to keep the redneck out of my voice at least 40 percent of the time, deliberately throwing in a "you guys" instead of a "y'all" at least once.

10) My waning faith in the quality of people in Los Angeles was fully restored.

That night, when I drove home, I had that reflex—a physical letting go of tenseness and nervous energy and fear—where you finally exhale. And then I immediately started wondering if I had been a dumbass and said anything really stupid. And then I thought about all the fun I'd had, and I was happy.

I was happy?

Me?

Yes. I was happy!

Chapter 15

• •

There is something to be said for making your home your refuge, your safe and centered space. Of course, if your house is stacked floor to ceiling with boxes still unpacked from your move several months ago, it is perhaps not the safe place you envision in your Howard Hughes fantasy. It's actually, really, incredibly cluttered. And *unsafe.*

Eventually I started unpacking, a box here, a pile there. While I may not have been the best math student on the planet, even I could see that the volume of stuff I had accumulated far exceeded the space I could afford to house it in.

I would have to pare down.

When I first moved into this house I was *so mad at Charlie.* We had lived in a big, huge, lofty condo in Studio City, big enough and more for all our stuff, and here I was stuck in this little spinster hovel with boxes and memories and copious cat hair.

But after a while I came to see that the real, physical constraints of my house were a blessing. I did not need this much crap. I had bought most of it on sale, any sale, and largely as a way to make me happy when I was a sad married housewife. I had shopped when we fought, I shopped when we weren't close,

I shopped when we weren't having sex, and really . . . *that is a lot of shopping.*

My new house could either be a big symbol of my failure (Falling down a rung! Or five!), or I could look at it as an opportunity to purge my life of collected bad memories.

I dealt with the easiest stuff first, the kitchen stuff. Kitchen gadgets and cookie sheets seemed to spring magically from the depths of my cabinets, stuffed in cupboards, spilling out of boxes. I didn't mind getting rid of the kitchenware because my husband had never fully appreciated my cooking adventures (his idea of a fine meal was ravioli from a can), and even on a good day my culinary skills left a little to be desired.

After several months of living alone, my cooking had deteriorated into a rapidly descending spiral of just plain pathetic. The day before I began my Great Kitchen Purge, my entire menu consisted of dry Cocoa Puffs, a turkey sandwich, three Red Vines, and a pickle—nary a pot nor plate was defiled. That is quite a feat!

On this particular Saturday of my First Decluttering, I had invited Jennifer over for dinner and needed to get into the kitchen and actually move without knocking over a pile or endangering a cat. I started paring down with the cookie sheets (Who needs seventeen half-rusted tin pans? Who?), moved on to the Tupperware (Is it truly necessary to maintain enough plastic to store a small family in, if cut in bite-size pieces?), and ended with the utensils. I do not know how I managed to accumulate four corkscrews, seven sets of tongs, and twenty-nine plastic corn holders shaped like little ears of corn. But no woman living alone really needs that much plastic corn.

After four hours of cleaning, unpacking, and sorting in the kitchen, I had managed to unload myself of two bags of trash (Pasta from 1997? Good-bye, old friend!) and three full boxes for Goodwill. It was a triumph of magical and also exhausting proportions. And Jennifer was arriving in approximately thirty-seven minutes for a home-cooked meal.

That evening I served her green bean casserole and tater tots. It was all I could work up. She arrived just as I once again successfully set off the fire alarm in my house with my exceptional cooking skills. But it led to a cooking catharsis of sorts as I finally discovered what the problem is: I suffer from Advanced Cooking ADD.

Cooking is an activity that requires constant supervision, and I tend to get distracted. Apparently, once I leave the kitchen, I completely forget that I even have a stove or a mystical "cooking room" in the house, and before long I am on the living room floor painting my toenails and watching *Entertainment Tonight* and also flipping through the mail, because I am a badass multitasker.

And then before you know it the alarm is going off and dinner is burned to a crisp. And *every single time this has ever happened,* which is a lot, I am completely shocked and freaked out when the alarm goes off. "Why is the smoke alarm going off? Is there a fire? Did someone break in? And start a fire? Why would someone do that?"

I'm not sure what was cathartic about that experience, except for finally being (self-)diagnosed with Cooking ADD. I also suffer from its closely related cousin affliction, Grocery Store Sensory Overload.

I know I should go to the grocery store instead of the 7-Eleven, but I can't be trusted in that place. Left to my own devices I will spend a hundred dollars and arrive home with items that when placed together do not even make one complete meal. I'll buy Shake 'n Bake but forget chicken, buy milk but forget cereal, buy lunch meat and no bread. It just happens. The grocery store is big and the selection is vast and I come down with a case of vertigo every time I walk through the perfectly oiled sliding glass doors.

And I love lists. I am a list-making fool. So I make lists for the grocery store on Post-it Notes, and on the back of the light bill, and even in a notebook bought solely for the purpose of holding my many lists. But even if the list makes it to the store (shocking rare incident, but it has happened), the list is not in the same order as the aisles, and I still have to walk around and everything is so pretty and appetizing and . . . look! Lucky Charms cereal! Lunchables with mini tacos! Oreos with chocolate filling! Hey, I'm an adult and what fun is it to be on your own and paying bills and doing things like wearing panty hose if you can't buy Oreos? I would be denying my power as an *adult* if I didn't buy these! It would be a travesty! In fact, by purchasing chocolate Double Stuf Oreos, I am declaring my independence!

And dammit if an hour later I'm not standing at the checkout with coffee filters, beer, four frozen Lean Cuisines, a big packet of Oreos, and seventeen other items that make no sense.

Cooking is overrated anyway. I cooked for my husband every day for years and years, and contrary to what we are all taught as little girls, the way to a man's heart is not through his stomach.

Or maybe it is, if you're a wonderful cook who manages to whip up masterful creations while wearing your high heels and your pearls. I myself was not really much of a whipper-upper. And Charlie's limited palate was a challenge, even for the best of cooks.

After he left, I tried to think of the one ingredient he hated above all else. After some serious contemplation of this matter, it arrived to me in a cabernet-infused moment of clarity: *scallions*. And I spent the next month committed to cooking only things that contained scallions, as if I could call forth my Inner Chef and Inner Woman Scorned and make them both happy with a wide variety of scallion-infused dishes.

It is surprising how many things you can add scallions to, like green bean casserole. And even tater tots, if you chop the scallions real small.

Chapter 16

. . . .

Days pass, and before long you find yourself adjusting to your new life even though you resisted so nobly at first. (And of course later you gave up noble altogether, along with your dignity, when you held up a bottle of wine at a dinner party and announced, "Y'all are all invited to my divorce!" then fled to the bedroom to cry, and later that evening pretended nothing at all had happened.) And by "you" I mean "me."

One step forward, one jagged half-step back.

Surprisingly, there were even times I found myself somewhere close to happy, small moments almost indiscernible.

One time it happened was on a Sunday afternoon. It was raining, always raining that spring, and I sat on my sofa in faded old pajamas and knitted through an entire Sunday afternoon watching exactly *zero* minutes of football. This is an important detail. For the duration of my marriage, I had been a football widow and loathed it. The TV would blare one sport or another every Sunday all day, and when I complained about it, Charlie just met up with a friend at a local sports bar to watch games in peace and with the added benefit of chicken wings.

Instead of Man Sports Programming, I selected a weepy, goofy movie from the 1970s, just the sort of thing to reverse the polarity of football. I popped popcorn and made coffee, and my cats all eventually gravitated to the couch. The house felt cozy instead of claustrophobic and I . . . *I was actually completely fine.* Alone.

It came as a shock.

I had no one to answer to but myself. No one to vacuum around, no one to make a meal for (other days I would bemoan this same fact, feel so sad and weepy because there was no one at all to serve dinner to, except the cats). I felt so untethered at first, after he left, without anyone to care for or fuss over or complain about. But on this day, I saw it was a freedom. No laundry to wash or fold, no one to shop for, no one to complain if the bathroom wasn't exactly sparkling or we were out of Diet Coke.

I sat there in my little rented house in Encino, and I knitted. Later I had a glass of wine on the patio, and for the first time since I had moved into that house, I stretched out on the chaise lounge and smiled, happy. I knew there would be more sadness ahead, because divorce was still looming and Lord, it was tiring. But this one day had been a perfect day, a small and quiet and perfect day, and I had actually had the presence of mind to recognize it.

It's progress. You take it where you can.

Chapter 17

· ·

Just a few weeks after my divorce papers had arrived, my boss suggested I take a personal day. This is what happens when you cry in a meeting. We were all sitting around the conference room table—me in my schlumpy "soon-to-be-divorced-woman" work uniform (black pants, unironed button-down blouse, Cardigan Of Constant Sorrow)—and discussing the redesign of a website.

I became rather more passionate than perhaps the moment warranted and found myself sniffling in front of a roomful of people. "That highlight color is *all wrong* and . . . and . . . it's so lonely, all by itself, with no high-contrast . . . and it's *alone* . . . with four cats . . . and it looks so sad . . . and and *I'm sorry*, I have to excuse myself. . . ."

These little crying episodes were just the icing on the crazy cake. It would happen at the strangest times, and try as I might, I couldn't predict what would set me off. I invested in waterproof mascara and Kleenex and hoped the uncontrollable tears would dry up soon.

One evening, Jennifer and I attended a going-away dinner for a friend of ours. The dinner was being held at Shannon's house, and I knew I would be able to knit there, and it was a very small crowd, and I couldn't *not* go to the very last, final good-bye party for a friend who was moving off to Montana.

Shannon, who was keenly aware of my isolationist tendencies, had insisted I attend. To be very honest I was happy enough, sitting on the sofa with Shan and two other close friends before the other partygoers arrived, knitting away on a mohair scarf. It was a simple drop-stitch thing but it was pretty, and people had complimented my handiwork.

We were all just talking and setting out plates of food and drinking wine and chitchatting, and somehow we got on the subject of birthdays.

"I'm going to cross a line next month," Amy said. "I'll be turning thirty, and I will no longer be in the eighteen-to-twenty-nine checkbox."

"There's not a checkbox for that," said Jennifer. "Is there?"

"I was filling out some kind of form the other day, and I noticed it," said Amy.

"Oh my God, I know!" said Shannon. "I was at the doctor's office the other day and I noticed there were all kinds of weird questions like that. And you know, when you get to the line about your marital status, there's 'single' and 'married' and also 'divorced.' Why can't they just have 'single' and 'married' on the form? Is 'divorced' important?"

It had not occurred to me that I myself would very soon cross into an entirely new category, one that had to be checked off on the eleventy million forms of my unforeseen future. And all of a sudden I burst into *crazy*.

It was a rather uncomfortable moment, as you can imagine. There I was at a party, a fun event in which people do not normally cry, and I was in a state. So I got up off the couch and ran away . . . to the balcony. At which time I discovered we were on the second floor, and *there was no escape from the balcony,* and I would have to one day, eventually, perhaps when I was old and gray and hunched over from living on the three-by-eight overhang, return to the party where I had just made an embarrassing mess of things and cried like a baby.

Yes.

So there I was, fully aware I'd just moved *way* down on the Party Guests We Must Invite To Stuff list, and it was starting to get kind of boring out there on the balcony and I was hungry, and the cake was indoors, and there really was no escape, even though I considered hoisting myself down onto the neighbor's balcony below, all *Mission Impossible* style, but I had on a skirt (and I was out of the clean, normal panties and so it was thong-up-the-butt day and that would not have been pretty). Finally there was nothing left to do but smoke a cigarette. Jennifer came out to assure me that there was no escape and she still loved me. And also they kind of needed the balcony for making the hot dogs. So could I please come inside and stop being crazy until everyone ate?

So I came out from hiding, and then we ate hot dogs and tried to pretend nothing happened. Later I checked my mascara in the bathroom mirror and it was still there, nary a smudge, held firmly in place by the sheer power of science and Maybelline.

Chapter 18

Stitch 'n Bitch became a fairly regular part of my new life. Since my job is downtown and I live way off in the Valley, it wasn't always easy to make it, but I tried to go as many Thursdays as I could.

I *loved* going to the knitting group. The knitters and crocheters I had met so far were nice, funny, kind, interesting, diverse, and smart. And no one was putting up a facade, or trying hard to be tragically hip, or looking over your shoulder as you talked to see if someone more interesting walked into the room. In *Los Angeles*. That was a miracle in itself.

And somewhere in me I had a deep need to bond socially with other women. I craved the company of girls, because there's something so rewarding about being in a room with women who have all these different perspectives and experiences and yarn.

Best of all, Stitch 'n Bitch was so much fun! Clearly, I don't have a *Sex and the City* life. I loathe bars. I'm bad in crowds, not good with meeting men, and even worse at trying to be desirable. It felt rare and special to meet a bunch of amazing women in a big social setting where no one was trying to pick up guys or get picked up, and I loved it. Which made me nervous.

Love hadn't really worked out for me so far.

The divorce kept chugging along, from a legal perspective. Fat envelopes of documents and equally fat lawyer bills would arrive with troubling regularity. We'd never fought in the past, me and Charlie. No reason to start bickering now just because of the divorce.

Sometimes I had been mad that we didn't fight much. Like I needed the drama of it, or maybe just the passion, any sign of passion.

In the evenings he came home like clockwork at half past seven. He would drop his keys in the nook by the front door, loosen his tie, and ask, "How was your day?" I sometimes thought about telling him, but then he would pick up the mail on the side table and flip through the bills. He would go to the bedroom to change clothes, and then he would come back downstairs in a faded, familiar T-shirt and some track pants and turn on the TV before walking into the kitchen to make a drink.

I wondered later if it all might have worked out if only we had argued once in a while, yelling and angry like couples in the movies, making up passionately afterward. (Do I even know what this mystical so-called make-up sex is?) Instead we were polite roommates who used to be fond of each other, but the years of dishes and bills and chicken noodle soup had dimmed whatever spark was there those first few years. I guess.

Maybe we had met as strangers and remained private and

solitary even against my every effort to get inside, figure us out, connect. I could tell Charlie anything; he was a good person and would try to listen—I knew that from the way he nodded in agreement as I talked about the new lamps I was thinking of for the bedroom, or the merits of running the A/C versus the ceiling fan. But somehow at the end of our marriage, we knew next to nothing about each other's thoughts or hopes or nightmares.

Sometimes it was a comfortable partnership, being married. There were no explanations, no dates, no failed attempts at romance. It was nice to come home every night to the same person, to something dependable.

And on other days, hot summer days when sweat pricked all over you even before morning, I wondered if my marriage wasn't some sedan, a trusty vehicle carrying me through life, keeping me a passenger forever. But it was safe. A safe sedan.

Chapter 19

. . . .

On an unexpected weekend outing, I went with Faith early one Saturday morning to the Hollywood Hills; she wanted to see the secret garden tucked away inside Beachwood Canyon. Faith is a woman I met at my knitting group, and we had become friends, and she knew me only in the context of who I was right then. It's an odd thought that you're making friends, and they only know you as the divorced woman, never knew Charlie, never knew you as a wife. It's a really liberating thought, too. You can be anyone you want to be. They see you as a whole woman, not half of a couple. That idea in itself gave me a little unexpected frisson of pleasure. While the friends you make in childhood are lovely, I often feel the ones I've made as an adult are more special because they are so rare. It's hard to find women friends in a mismatched, spread-out place like Los Angeles, and I was lucky to have her.

We found the garden and walked around for an hour and later had lunch at a quiet outdoor Mexican restaurant back in the Valley. We were just talking and something she'd said or something I'd remembered made my eyes well up. I hated it when that happened, and I tried to turn my head, think of funny jokes, hoped she hadn't seen it.

"After my close friend Jeff died," said Faith, "I saw a counselor. It helped."

I looked at her for a minute. I wasn't sure how to tell her that
I just wasn't ready yet to sift through the rubble of the past; I
needed maybe a to-do list, something with bullet points, a road
map would be just fine. But the idea of launching into therapy at
that moment was too much for me; I was having a hard enough
time waking each day and waiting until 7:00 PM to drink, usually
a good cabernet. Probably I shouldn't mention that. Probably
that is a sign you should actually run, not walk, to a counselor.

Later when I was back at my little house I sat out on the patio
and had a glass of wine; it was past 7:00 PM after all. My neighbors were having a birthday party for . . . a grandson? Nephew,
maybe. I could hear them all evening, playing salsa music, welcoming family and friends as they arrived, talking on cell phones,
discussing the food, playing basketball, children shrieking, running, laughing, the thump of the bat on the piñata, the cheers of
the adults, the shouting and laughter when someone opened it
up, the candy and toys spilling out onto the concrete driveway.
One of the kids stumbled and fell and cried, but all the adults
rushed over with soothing words and someone must have handed
the baby a piece of candy from the piñata. The crying slowed to
little gulps and the chattering resumed, the music got changed to
a different song, this one a little older, everything in Spanish
sounding more like a song for the grown-ups. They brought out
the cake and everyone laughed and clapped and talked over each
other.

I hear the sounds of life from my neighbors. From my house

they hear the dryer, maybe, tumbling a load of towels, or perhaps the clink of glasses in the sink as I finally wash three weeks of dirty dishes (sad to say in all that time, the only things piled up to wash were the wineglasses, a few forks, and the cat food bowl).

Hearing them laugh, live, love, talk, and eat made me lonely and comforted. My neighbors were nice people, simple good people, hardworking (I don't know her name, she's a hairdresser, the husband a landscaper), with two daughters; one just bought the house across the street. The husband next door called his wife "Mama," and it was endearing and sexy all at the same time, not the least bit creepy the way it seems on paper in words.

It is peculiar to be in your mid-thirties, becoming more divorced by the minute, and trying to figure out who you are as a person. Thinking back on your life and trying to pinpoint exactly where you turned left, detoured, went too fast or not fast enough. Remembering every kiss you'd ever had. Remembering the first time you let a boy go to first base. Remembering why it was so important for you to be married, always married.

But when it's late and the whole neighborhood is dark and the party next door has ended, sleep feels a million miles away, so I just give up and bring the bottle of wine out to the patio with me, and try to picture where it is that my life went ass over teakettle, about as far off the road map as one can get.

I once had a very clear picture of who I was and what my life looked like. Then it was gone and I had no idea what my future would look like, and it terrified me. (Sometimes it also exhilarated me, like when I imagined myself living someplace that is larger than eight hundred square feet, and is maybe on a beach, or in a villa in some rolling, sweeping countryside, and often this fantasy is filled with a man who looks *exactly* like Gregory Peck in *To Kill a Mockingbird*. And we have a kid named Scout, or a dog, but either way something small and cute is named Scout. And I wear really nice dressing gowns. There might be wine involved in these fantasies.)

For as long as I could remember, I was so sure of my role and my path. My entire life had been a series of plot points on a map, carefully charted out by generations of women before me who loved their families, took care of the husbands and children (always plural), kept a good house, and made excellent fried chicken and homemade biscuits. I remember looking at my Oma's delicate, floury hands one afternoon when she showed me how to make fried pies. I was six or seven years old, and we were visiting her in Corpus Christi for Easter weekend.

"You remember this, now: when you crimp the edges down with a fork, it makes a perfect little pie."

She was showing me how to form the saucer-sized rounds of pie dough into half-moons filled with peach preserves or apricot. The whole kitchen was filled with her cooking, and it was warm and cozy.

"One day when you have a granddaughter of your own, you'll pass this on to her, too." She kissed me on the forehead, left a flour handprint on my fat little cheek. She smelled lovely, like sugar and menthol cigarettes and apricot, and I loved her.

I remember that moment as clear as if it happened yesterday. I always just assumed I would one day have a granddaughter to make fried pies with, although deep-fried dough made entirely of flour and Crisco has likely gone out of style. I don't even know if you can buy Crisco in California, unless they make it out of flaxseeds or soy.

Oh, Lord. I never for a minute thought I'd be this woman sitting alone in her thirties with a bottle of rather inexpensive red wine and a patina of cat hair on her pajamas and four half-finished knitted scarves in varying shades of orange. Alone. Looking backward to see what might be ahead.

I always suspected I had to be half of something.

I was wrong.

Chapter 20

· ·

I picked so carefully. I am one who chooses from a wide array of options. I like to see things, feel them out, touch and smell and use all that superstitious intuition to find a perfect fit. I love my gut feelings.

I thought I chose a man who was solid and stable and genuinely seemed to love me. I didn't rush into anything, in fact I had spent years and years looking for him, The One. I probably began searching for The Man I Would Marry even before I was old enough to date. I hadn't been impetuous like some of my girlfriends and married right out of high school, even though I was madly in love with my sweetheart, Matt. He was the first one I surrendered to, and handed over "my power" to, and it was love, and I was addicted.

During my whole senior year at Central High, I spent Study Hall writing little poems using words I didn't really understand to describe him. One day those poems will probably be discovered in a shoebox in someone's attic and the discoverer of such a fine treasure will have a hearty laugh over them.

I was perhaps a little on the wordy side. And I was passionate! My thesaurus became my confidante, and I would write tortuously crafted stanzas and sometimes I would send him notes during sixth period that described my love for him. After school, we spent long afternoons driving in his orange Volkswagen Beetle or walking in the woods behind his house, talking about the future. Matt was an artist; he could sketch out intricate portraits in minutes, on napkins and postcards and sometimes on the back of my hand. Matt smoked cigarettes and wore Eau de Grey Flannel.

"I want to draw what's in my head and . . . and draw you . . . and sell my sketches and have people ask about my work," said Matt. Inhaling on a Camel unfiltered.

"I want to be the girl in your pictures," I said.

It wasn't that I lacked goals as a teenager. I had goals. For one thing, I wanted out of that small town so bad I could taste it, and I read everything I could get my hands on, especially books about foreign countries, or women writers, or anything and everything having to do with travel. My father was a newspaperman and had been one since the day I was born, so I grew up reading the paper cover to cover each day, a habit I cannot let go of even now when the Internet makes news available all day and your fingers never get inky. I could always recite a hundred useless facts, but I learned early on that in my small town, the line between "smart" and "snotty" was a fine one, which basically meant that you knew the answer but kept your mouth shut if you wanted folks to like you.

And Lord, how I did want people to like me. I was born a people-pleaser. Maybe it's deep in my genetic code, all those women making fried pies and homemade meals for families the size of a squadron. Nothing felt better than a smile of approval, a nod of acknowledgment that you'd done well.

Except love.

In my defense, it wasn't just my insatiable need for love that plotted my course on the map of my life. Getting married was what you *did*. When you no longer had school to measure yourself by and the patterns of your life stretched out ahead, the next logical step was to get married and settled down. And so I set out to be married and check off the last box on life's to-do list. I had a hundred years of female programming in my veins, and even when I knew there were other choices, other paths women could choose to take, I wanted marriage because it felt right and comfortable. I loved that picture! I loved the Donna Reed apron and the homemade meals we'd have in our kitchen. And I'd be a kind but firm mother and teach them the value of a dollar, like my folks had taught me, and I'd pass along fried pie recipes and a love of reading the newspaper.

God, I wanted that life. My picture was clear and lovely: Get married, settle down, have a family. Be happy.

I only got as far as the marriage itself. We walked down that aisle, and I knew he was The One. But settling down was harder to do. And neither Charlie nor I were ready for children, especially at first, and during the days (or weeks, or months) when I found myself imagining chubby infant hands and baby clothes, I just stayed quiet and kept taking my birth control pills religiously. Later, when we stopped having sex altogether, I still took a pill each day as if that in itself would ward off unwanted baby dreams.

I have no idea what dreams to ward off now. I have no idea what the new picture looks like. Thirty-something years old seems like a very peculiar time to figure out who you are.

Chapter 21

. . . .

Spring was coming. The night was breezy and my wind chimes were humming.

"Maybe if I ate something I'd feel better."

I sat on the patio in sock feet, sipping a nice, sturdy cabernet, wondering what might be hiding in the pantry and if it could be microwaved or covered in cheese. And I started thinking about what I had eaten during that day. Usually I tried not to dwell on such things, as I had plenty else to ponder, such as impending insanity and an escalating laundry crisis, but before long I was writing down every single thing I had consumed in the past twenty-four hours. I then did the Evil Math and I discovered something interesting: On that particular day, a very average day in my life, I had ingested 60 percent of my daily calories from wine. The other 40 percent? That came from jalapeño potato chips and French fries.

Apparently, I was on the wine and fried potato diet.

When most folks go through a divorce they join gyms and go on diets and lose weight; I guess that's what they refer to as The Divorce Diet. It's all about looking your best in the face of

. . . . .

adversity because getting thin is the best revenge. Me? I am apparently revenge free.

I gained . . . many pounds. Multiples of pounds. And I worked my fatness into conversation, as if by acknowledging it I could minimize it. (I couldn't.) As in, "Well, y'all know, I don't like those small claustrophobic yarn shops because I'm fat and might knock something over like a bull in a china shop. Watch out, here comes my ass!"

It was a weird way of claiming something, out loud, before someone else did. I pointed out The Obvious before others got a chance to mention it. This was Defensive Driving 101, as applied to weight gain.

I wished it weren't the case. Because as much as I like my new philosophy of living life all truthful and honest and crazy, I'd have preferred to keep The Fat a secret. It felt sort of shameful, like my body had become a physical testament to my unhappiness, my sadness, my loss.

Well, you don't need a Ph.D. and a couch to figure that one out.

In the last year of marriage, it seemed like the more I tried to hold on to Charlie, the further away he got. But I did my best to keep up the smiling facade with my friends and family, never once letting on that my marriage was falling apart. I was so good at hiding and lying—to myself and others—and pretending. Of course, when you get divorced people start to figure out that maybe it wasn't Leave-It-to-Beaver-land at your house. But if you don't talk about it, that shameful word *divorce,* neither will they. *Weight is a totally different ball game.*

I have struggled with my weight my whole life. Not a little

five- or ten-pound struggle, but the true gain/lose-forty-pounds-a-year struggle. I wish it were a private battle, like scabies or acid reflux. But with weight you can't hide your issue. You can't say to folks you haven't seen in a while, "Oh yeah! That? It's not my ass. I am just hauling around a compost heap for a friend. Junk in the trunk, ha ha!" Or "Oh! Don't think I've become fat. No, no. I haven't. What you see there is just my polar insulation. I'm very cold in the new office and need seventy-two layers of clothes to keep warm."

So, you know, people can tell. They can see Fat.

Even so, there's also something comforting about being heavier. It's no coincidence that I gained weight when I most needed some protection from the world. I wanted to minimize myself, seem smaller somehow, and what better way to become unseen than to gain weight? People's eyes pass right over you; men pay less attention to you. I wish it weren't true because it's so unfair, and yet at the same time, I used it to my advantage, building a wall of fat and insulation against the world, against rejection, against lonely.

It was easy to say to myself, "I'll think about dating when the sun explodes, or maybe when I lose a little weight." It became an invisible benchmark for the day, some far-off time in the future, when I might be ready to get close to someone again.

My little divorce diet of 60 percent wine, 40 percent "other" couldn't have been healthy. Well, except for the wine part. Jennifer and I like to find new and exciting studies on the Internet that prove wine has amazing health benefits. We are forever e-mailing each other new studies we discover on the

Internet, stories about researchers who have just discovered some previously unknown compound in alcohol that makes you happy or live longer, or enhances libido in test crickets. I believe all these studies prove one thing, and that is how much scientists love their libation. Bless their hearts.

I knew I should go on a diet. Not because I wanted Charlie back, or because I thought I had to be skinny to find a new man. But I knew I couldn't live forever on a gallon of wine and jalapeño potato chips. And I couldn't fit into any of my clothes, and I genuinely wanted to shove a Snickers bar into the face of the next ninety-seven-pound girl who told me she's fat. Obviously, this was not a healthy response. And I couldn't go to jail for assault with a deadly Snickers bar because I'd look horrible in prison-issue orange.

Deep down inside, I knew it wasn't about picking a diet or counting or measuring so that I could learn the proper way to eat. Any woman who has ever had a weight problem usually knows more about dieting and food and calories than anyone else you'll ever meet. We know exactly what to do, *we just don't do it*.

But being overweight wasn't giving me the payoff it once did. Or, more specifically, I realized that it was no longer good for me to be bad to myself.

So, I *contemplated* reworking the potato and wine diet I'd been on those many months—not to embark upon some crazy grapefruit and meatballs diet—just your basic "eat something other than McDonald's" strategy. I decided to incorporate some of the "eat a vegetable that isn't fried" plan as well. My goal was to get the wine down to a healthy 10 percent of calories. If the planets aligned *just so,* I was going to perhaps, *maybe* exercise. Mostly I was just going to work on not feeling so bad about my body.

Tomorrow was another day. And if that day ended in too many glasses of red wine or an hour crying on the bathroom floor or a whole row of purl when I should have knitted, then it was just another reason to look forward to the next day.

Tomorrow was the day when nutritious diets began, and plans started, and scarves got knit anew, and the first day of the rest of my whole damn life would begin.

## Part 3

Joining Pieces Together

Chapter 22

. . . .

Spring evaporated in a string of hundred-degree days, and I had to crank up the air-conditioning to knit. I feared my electric bills to come. I switched from wine to chilled beer . . . *light* beer. Of course.

I was invited to a birthday party for my dear friend Amber at a club near the beach in Venice. As soon as I heard the word *club* I shrank back into myself. I would not be attending such an event.

Jennifer had a different plan in mind for me.

"I'm coming to your house to pick you up at eight," she said. "I expect you to be ready. It will be fun! You remember fun? You used to like it."

"I can always drive to meet you there," I suggested.

"No way," said Jennifer. She knew me well enough to know that was my covert way of slinking out of an obligation. "Amber is our friend, and she loves you and comes to your house all the time, and this is her birthday. The least you can do is go for a few hours and have a glass of wine and try to smile, for her sake."

So I agreed, even though I felt about a hundred years old, fat and washed-up, and terribly, terribly almost-divorced.

The Friday night before the party, I sat on the sofa with *Jaws* on the television and knitted up a little bracelet bag. I wanted a teensy, cute handbag to take out to the club with just enough room for my ID, lipstick, small compact, money, and keys. This bag needed to be something tiny and decorative that could stay on my body as the night and cocktails wore on, since I tend to be both extremely paranoid about losing my handbag and also extremely ditzy and forgetful that I even *own* a handbag.

Plus, I wanted something to do that night, the night before the party, keeping my hands busy so I wouldn't fidget and find excuses for ditching Amber's birthday celebration. By the time Richard Dreyfuss and Roy Scheider were paddling back to Amity Island, I was done with all the knitting, including sewing the sides up. I felted it the next morning, and sewed on the bracelet bangles. It looked good, I had to admit. Perfect for a night out on the town.

I had not been to a club in years. I used to go out a lot back when I was married, all the time in fact. I'd get the girls together and drag them off to some salsa club or another. But it had been a l-o-n-g time since I'd gone out on the town. I had to sit myself down prior to the evening and have a come-to-Jesus with myself. I never feel really comfortable in these very-Los-Angeles places, where all the women are stick-thin and beautiful and enhanced and dressed in tiny scraps of clothing. In fact, I avoid these scenes as much as possible.

But it was Amber's birthday and I was going to this place, so I might as well shut up and move on and have a decent attitude about the whole thing. I believe in kindergarten this is what we call an "attitude adjustment," and I was in dire need of one. Nothing is more exhausting and awful than going out and feeling bad about it the whole time. It doesn't just ruin your night, it bleeds into others' experiences and they can feel it radiating off you, like stink waves or something.

I didn't want to have stink waves of self-loathing and sadness.

Saturday night came and I pulled on my one most flattering pair of jeans, blow-dried my hair, and put on some mascara. I practiced a smile. I practiced a hair flip. I felt like an idiot.

But so what if I was going to stand in a roomful of women whose entire bodies could be eclipsed by my left thigh? If I were going to be standing there, I might as well stand tall. I wore three-inch heels. Jennifer saw me and smiled.

"You look great!" she said. "Wow, and tall, too! This is going to be a superfun night, you'll see."

Then she hurried me out the door before I could change my mind or my shoes.

We met Amber at the club and got introduced to a huge group of her friends, people I'd never met before. I smiled and did not perform any hair flips. I could feel fear and acute self-consciousness pooling up inside me, and all my muscles were tense, ready for rejection. I looked around the room. I was probably the only larger-than-size-six girl in the whole club, but I felt tall in my three-inch heels. I loved my friends, and Jennifer held on to my hand, and we ordered champagne, and I breathed. In and out. Exhale. *Relax.*

And I did. I relaxed.

Every time I caught myself staring at some impossibly thin

girl in a three-inch-square scrap of fabric masquerading as a skirt, I just let it go. I even surprised myself, to be honest. I figured I'd have at least one freak-out moment, but I didn't. I had fun, I got to see a few people I hadn't visited with in ages, and the music was good. I didn't dance, but I did a lot of people-watching, a lot of nodding along to half-heard conversations, and chimed up in many birthday toasts for the birthday girl. I pretended, for one whole night, that I was just a regular girl in the crowd, a normal girl like any other.

Maybe that's what you do in this life, just pretend you're okay. You tell yourself to stop thinking of every single way the night will go wrong and you put on clothes and arrange your face in a smile, and before long you feel a real smile replacing the fake one. You do things even though they scare you. Maybe before long, you end up being the comfortable-in-your-skin person you're pretending to be.

I hope so, anyway.

The bracelet bag was a big hit, too. Three girls asked me where I got it, and I didn't lose my lipstick or keys all night long.

Chapter 23

. . . .

After the success of Amber's birthday party, I decided to have my own birthday party.

It would be my very first birthday party since the seventh grade! That's right, I had not had a big birthday party of people (other than family) since I was thirteen years old. And we weren't allowed to get rowdy intoxicated or smoke or cuss back then, so this would be a definite improvement over junior high.

I invited my friends and some of the folks I had met through my Stitch 'n Bitch group to the shindig. Jennifer almost fell over from the shock of me—me!—hosting a party and inviting real live humans. I almost fell over from the shock of pre-birthday-party stress that took place. I cleaned my house for two days and there was still a mountain of boxes in the office, towering over everything. Plus, Jen had to come over early and help me clean since I spent so much time focusing on arranging the patio that I completely forgot that rooms such as the kitchen and the bathroom needed a scrubbing.

At 3:00 PM, one hour before the party officially began, I had to make an emergency run to the grocery store—not even the 7-Eleven, the *real* grocery store—for dip, ice, and last-minute supplies. But apparently a clerk at the store forgot to put the bag containing the dip and salsa in my buggy, and I left the store with no chip accoutrements whatsoever, a fact I did not realize until 4:15. And then I realized, "Oh my God, it's 4:15!" I was still grimy from house-cleaning and in desperate need of a bath. When my first guests arrived, I was still in the shower. Hi, guests! Excuse my bad hostessing, I have been vacuuming for your convenience and I have to go get dressed now!

Gwen and Carrie, two of my new knitting friends, graciously offered to go to the store and repurchase the dip and salsa. Gwen gave me a little hug and whispered, "Don't worry! Your house looks great and hey . . . happy birthday!"

I took a deep breath and tried to relax. *Relax. It's just a little birthday party.* Guests started arriving and they brought all sorts of food and drinks, which was a really *really* good thing, as I had a small bit of trouble with grilling the hamburgers.

I had carefully seasoned and prepared four pounds of ground beef and shaped them into perfect patties, laid out on a cookie sheet and separated with sheets of heavy-duty tinfoil. All this Betty Crockeresque food prep was for naught, however, since I dropped the hamburgers before they even made it to the grill.

Yeah, that's right. I dropped *all of them.*

In my defense, it was not entirely my fault. The barbecue grill is ancient, and it kind of leans to one side or the other depending on how it feels that day, and as I set the huge tray of uncooked burgers on the wooden shelf attached to the side of the grill, the whole thing shifted and they went sliding off in some kind of Horror Movie Barbecue scene. There was much shrieking and gasping and shock all around. I almost cried, but Shannon saved the day and did some necessary rinsing.

Yes, we washed off the burgers and cooked them anyway.

And we ate them.

Later, Jennifer decided to "help" me barbecue. So she poked and prodded around on the grill (complaining the whole entire time about how awful hard it was to barbecue and how damn hot it was in the Valley), and she perhaps poked or prodded a hot dog or two into the burning charcoal. But, to her credit, she did not drop all of them like some people.

We all sat outside on the patio and ate "ground" burgers and well-charred hot dogs, and my friends, a mix of new and old, sang "Happy Birthday" to me, and we toasted the evening repeatedly. I do believe at some point I stood up and said, "Y'all are all invited to my divorce!" and instead of the deathly pall of divorce silence creeping across the crowd, everyone just laughed and ate cake, and I only tried to hide from the party once, which is a success in my world.

Chapter 24

. . . .

The more I climbed out of my shell and started socializing, little by little, the more people started hinting that it was time for me to start dating. I wasn't sure what almanac they consulted for this gem of advice, but my inner timetable didn't exactly have the same milestone inked on the calendar. I had a hard time imagining ever feeling close to anyone again.

Charlie, on the other hand, moved in with another woman. His almanac was obviously set on Leap Year. Shannon was the one who confirmed it for me, through the friend-of-a-friend grapevine, even though I'd suspected it for a while. The news about Charlie and his rapid pace of "moving on" made my reluctance to date seem even stranger to people.

I secretly wondered what she looked like, if they were happy, what they talked about. I was aware of the new addition, Creepy Ex-Wife, to my list of fine attributes, such as cat lady, crazy, and also spinster knitter. But I couldn't help it. I'm a naturally curious person. It made me an excellent competitor in junior high science fairs.

I didn't know where they lived or who she was. The friend-of-a-friend grapevine was surprisingly unforthcoming on details. I suspected they were trying to spare me worse heart-break and crazy. What they didn't know, of course, is that as a fine specimen of Basic Garden Variety Woman, I would just make up the details in my own mind. Loneliness does wreak havoc on your imagination.

Charlie was sitting at their new house right that very minute, on the computer answering e-mails, maybe drinking a rum and Coke. Maybe she was making dinner. Nothing with too many ingredients, no mushrooms or tomatoes or a heavy sauce; he may have changed his address and his marital status and his lover, but some things never change.

To know someone that well is hard work. I couldn't see myself putting in the effort again.

Maybe things would change.

Maybe he pretended to like tomatoes now.

Chapter 25

. . . .

After a few weeks consulting with my divorce lawyer and receiving his bills in the mail at an alarmingly regular pace, I came to a conclusion.

I had made a terrible vocational error.

I myself did not have a job in which we had these mystical things called "billable hours" by which you could legally charge someone for a phone call. It was shocking. I had heard stories, of course, folks who'd been dragged through divorce and all the jokes that came with it: "Love is grand, divorce is twenty grand," and "Know why divorce is so expensive? Because it's worth it."

Well, at least I could make jokes about it later. That was, if I weren't living in a cardboard box with four cats and eleven pairs of shoes by the end of this thing.

Before I had chosen a lawyer of my very own to pay and pay and pay some more, I had asked friends and even my boss for advice on lawyer friends. Did they know anyone who'd had a good divorce lawyer? The answer was always about the same. Apparently, people don't have a really high feeling of love and trust for their divorce lawyers. In fact, some of the words I heard used to describe their experiences made my hair stand up on end.

Some made me blush, and I am not a woman prone to blushing when it comes to salty language.

Clearly, divorce was not for the faint at heart, or the broken-hearted, or the just plain broke.

I will be the first to admit that prior to my divorce I was not the most fiscally responsible person on the planet. Whenever my financial outlook is particularly uncertain, I have the uncontrollable urge to shop. I can only assume this is a plot hatched by the government and key retail establishments (mainly anyone who sells cute shoes), and they have implanted some sort of reverse financial homing device in my brain. I bet all those years of getting salmon to swim upstream was just a beta test.

Getting married did not necessarily up my financial know-how. In fact, I would say it sent me back about a hundred years. I must be a social throwback. At any moment I'm just going to show up in a hoopskirt and corset because as embarrassing as it is to admit, I just assumed that I would be married and happy my whole life and have some nice manly man there to do the bills and paperwork-filing and insurance and evil taxes and so on. In return I'd be real pretty and work hard and do the cleaning and cooking, and we'd all have kids named John Boy and be living on Tara.

That did not happen. And it wasn't as horribly one-sided as it sounds, throwing all the financial burden on my husband. In my defense, I kept my end of the bargain, worked some long hours, did laundry like no tomorrow, and made amazing fried chicken on occasion. And I did indeed provide value in areas that we will not detail here because my parents might one day read this.

Also, in my defense, I am a dumbass.

All people, even those who have been caught in embarrassing photos with hoopskirts over their heads, need to be intimately involved in their financial well-being, and that is a fact. Take it from me, a cautionary tale. I had no idea what the total of my personal debt was. All the bills and how exactly to tackle the debt—it was scary and depressing and looming up at night in the form of this: a nightmare in which I and the cats were forced to live in a storage shed in North Hollywood and eat beans out of a can. And in this nightmare, I am surrounded by boxes of cute shoes that I cannot wear anywhere 'cause no one invites me to things anymore because I live in a storage unit with four cats and my imaginary friend named Bloomingdales who tells me about new shoes I can never afford to buy.

And there are bugs.

But once the whole singleness and spinster life and so on began to sink in, and once I began receiving bills from the afore-mentioned divorce lawyer, I decided that someone had to bring home the Meow Mix and cute shoes, and so of course I called a house meeting. Unable to convince the four cats to go out and find gainful employment, I decided I must have a *plan* and this *plan* was to (1) Find out how much debt I was actually in and (2) Figure out how *not* to be in debt my whole life. And also get a checkbook.

It would be hard to believe I worked at a bank, wouldn't it?

Before the spinsterdom, I never needed to know what any-body at the bank was talking about since I was an artist, and they can't tell a pixel from a pigeon, and it all worked just fine. But I suddenly had a grave need to know what goes on in checkbooks and bill paying and high interest rates, and luckily at the bank there are all sorts of people who know about money and banking (No way! Y'all come bank here! We know about banking!), and it occurred to me I might be able to ask questions, financial questions, and no one would be the least bit surprised or offended because I used a Ziploc baggie as my change purse. These people really know their stuff and love to talk about banking.

So I picked some brains and learned some stuff and I put all my bills in a room, and one long afternoon I had a party with some wine and a calculator and made up a newfangled thing these banking folks call "a budget."

According to mystical lore, "the budget" is a tool for tracking every single thing you make or spend. It's a simple tally of what comes in and what goes out. And it works! You don't even really need a computer program. You can scribble it on the back of your electric bill or on a plain old piece of notebook paper. And it's much like making a list, and lists are of course the elixir of life, so there's something strangely satisfying about it once you stop crying.

I was too scared at first to even know how much debt I had. Sure, I had a pretty general idea ("general" meaning "a whole lot of debt" and "maybe I will cry" and "is there any ice cream?"), but I did not know the *actual* amount. And that is sad. So once I wrote down every bill and expense and credit card, I had a full picture of my finances. I looked through old receipts to figure out how much I spent a month on groceries and my illicit runs to the 7-Eleven. I factored in pet food, gas, and so on, and then measured that against how much I bring in each month.

It wasn't a pleasing picture. In fact, it required fortification of the chardonnay grape variety. I was shocked and appalled at how much money I in fact *did not have*. At that point in the budgeting process, I maybe needed to stand up and walk around for a few minutes and regroup. (*Regroup* is a term I have learned that means "keep from running out in your nightgown and directing traffic while wearing your bra on your head.") It is important, when going through a divorce and analyzing your finances, to regroup from time to time.

After the initial shock wore off, I was actually relieved. After all the years of being in the dark about our shared marital finances, and after all the months of purposely refusing to face up to my own adult picture of fiscal doom, I finally knew what I was up against. My looming financial ruin was less creepy and scary, since my real financial ruin was neatly laid out in numbers on paper. Something about knowing a thing, the full extent of a thing, feels closer to freedom.

For the first time in my adult life, through the fairy-tale world of Budgeting, I even figured out ways I could save money (like bringing my breakfast and lunch to work, and not shopping at the 7-Eleven for groceries, and so on), and it felt liberating to be 100 percent totally in the know about my money. It was still depressing as all get out, but as any Southerner who has lived through numerous Civil War Battle Reenactments will tell you: The key to success in life is just having a plan. Because if you do not have a plan, you will be reconstructing that battle 'til the day you die.

Charlie had made all the decisions thus far; he had decided to leave, when to move out, when to file for divorce, even where our divorce would be settled. Taking control of my own monetary future felt like the biggest step yet on the path to self-sufficiency. It was the first time in months that I was actually taking charge of my life. Taking responsibility. At first, I had drifted along in my fog of sheer agony, and later in a dense state of denial, or misplaced hope. But as they say, hope is not a plan. Wishing is not a plan. Bemoaning is not a plan, though it sure feels good to complain and pitch a hissy fit sometimes, and occasionally cry in a corner dramatically.

The only real plan is one where you take a problem by the horns and write it down on paper, even if it's just on the back of your electric bill. A list is a plan. A budget is a plan. And a plan will set you free.

Chapter 26

· ·

The new budget had a strange effect on me.

Before I spent that weekend analyzing my bills and figuring out how I would ever afford to pay the lawyer, I used to hide from the mail. A fat packet of legal documents would arrive once a week or so, and it all felt overwhelming and exhausting. But something changed once I got ahold of myself financially. I stopped hiding from the mail.

I also stopped feeling like I was spiraling out of control, toward some grim future that was going to be forever in peril, always a day late and a hundred dollars short.

By then I was fully entrenched in the divorce process and there was not going to be any turning back. That much was certain. With my one small triumph in facing my money fears, I managed to get a foothold on my new life.

Up until that point I had only seen the divorce for all the things it was stealing from me, sucking out my perfect picture for my life and creating an empty place so deep and wide inside me that I closed in on myself. Getting divorced meant that I was losing my safety net in a million and one ways. My social safety net was gone. As half of a couple, my role was pretty clear in polite society. There's a certain confidence, a *solidity* conferred on you when you get that ring on your hand. I felt it slipping away from me. Being a divorced woman, or even a single woman, does not feel the same as being married did. Especially when you're new to it.

There's the money safety net. Two incomes are certainly easier to live on than one. And since my job had always been "secondary income," I made less money than he did. I struggled with things I'd let him handle in years past, like car insurance and health insurance and veterinarian bills.

And there's the safety net of togetherness. When you're married you're not alone. You come home at night to someone, you have someone to remember to tell that joke to, you have someone to blame for the weird stain on the rug. I started blaming the cats, of course, but it wasn't nearly as satisfying. Sometimes the aloneness would creep in and take me by surprise.

Then I made that budget.

It's such a small thing in retrospect. But I got the first shiver of accomplishment I'd had in months. I was proud of myself, I felt cautiously optimistic. Pulling out of debt and paying for this new life of mine was a challenge, no doubt. And I felt fully, finally, totally capable of it . . . cautiously, at least.

It made me wonder what else I was capable of, if only I'd set my mind to it, concentrate, and make a plan. After all, I was going to come through the other end of this thing. People do. It was the first time I began to wonder who I would be on the other side. What kind of woman would I be? What did I want for my life?

Chapter 27

Envelopes kept arriving in the mail, a court date was set, and I started planning ahead, calling all my friends and asking them to come with me to the hearing, asking for the day off work, and most importantly, making frantic last-minute calls of desperation to Aharon, my hairdresser.

Aharon is magic. With a little hair dye, styling products, and some intense blow-drying, he can transform me from frumpy to pretty in under two hours' time, a miracle if ever there was one. He's Israeli and has a lilting, exotic accent, and he even has an assistant. This is apparently quite common at fancy-pants Beverly Hills salons, a far cry from the home perms of my youth, in which my seven-year-old brother was the assistant to the stylist, my mom (with very poor results, I might add). It's so much fun to live in a city like Los Angeles where you can pretend to be a Beverly Hills "I get my hair done here" kind of girl, even if just for a few hours. It's like playing dress-up, except a tiny bit more expensive. I'd had to make a whole line in the budget just for my haircutting needs.

I love Aharon because he knows I must have boundaries and tough love. This was apparent when I called him two days before my appearance in divorce court. I was in absolute emotional meltdown and I needed help. Hair help.

"Umberto Beverly Hills, reservation desk. How can I help you?"

"Hi," I said. "Can I speak with Aharon? Please? I have a hair emergency."

"Just one moment," said the receptionist. "I'll see if he's with a client."

Interestingly enough, the receptionist did not bat an eye at my melodramatics. They must get hair emergency phone calls on a regular basis. After a few minutes on hold, Aharon picked up the line.

"Hello?"

"Aharon, it's me, Laurie. I have a hair emergency."

"What happened . . . ?" he asked. "Are you okay? Did you get cake in your hair?"

"Cake?"

"It happened to one of my clients before," said Aharon. "Blue frosting, it was terrible!"

"No," I said. Thrown off-kilter for a minute. Who knew the secret dilemmas of hair stylists!

"Well, thank God, because the cake is very hard on the hair. We had to cut," said Aharon.

"Aharon, please . . . I have an emergency," I said. Whispered. "Yes?"

"I need bangs."

"Absolutely not," said Aharon. I had never heard him use that tone of voice with me before.

"Aharon, *I need bangs*," I said. Sometimes you just have to be firm with folks.

"Okay, tell me the truth. What's going on?" he asked.

"I have to go to divorce court, and I am scared, and I need bangs!" Finally, there. I said it.

"Laurie," he said, "you cannot solve this problem with bangs. Now be good, come see me soon. Do not ask me about the bangs for at least six more months." And with that he hung up.

It was sad, really, having my hair emergency dismissed in such a manner. But in the end, he was right. You cannot solve a problem like divorce with bangs.

Chapter 28

· ·

𝒯𝒽𝑒 𝒹𝒾𝓋𝑜𝓇𝒸𝑒 𝒽𝑒𝒶𝓇𝒾𝓃𝑔 𝓉𝑜𝑜𝓀 place in a small room, and I had Jennifer and Shannon and Rebecca to hold me up in case I had some kind of embarrassing falling-down incident. I was mighty nervous. It would be the first time I had seen Charlie face-to-face since the day he moved out. Even though the hottest of the weather had passed already, I had broken a sweat that morning just trying to get my panty hose on. I was also wearing very high heels and a little too much makeup, my mask for the day.

And my lawyer was there, of course. Costing me money with every passing second.

I expected to feel a lot of emotions, seeing Charlie for the first time in so long. I expected to be overcome by morose crying, or feel sadness and loss, but we just said "Hi" to each other, like polite strangers, and all of us walked inside the courthouse. As soon as we entered the courtroom, however, I was indeed strongly filled with emotion.

The emotion of *horror*.

Clearly, I had to be in the wrong courtroom. This couldn't possibly be family court, could it? Perhaps the judge had mistakenly lumped us in with the criminal court and we were mixed in with the felons and carjackers?

I saw the frightened looks on my girlfriends' faces as well, so I turned to my lawyer, whispering for discretion.

"Are we in the right place?" I asked. "These people look . . . homicidal."

"Oh, we're in the right place," he assured me.

There was a man in a full-body cast, wheeled in by his attorney. A woman in high-high heels was wearing the tiniest rhinestone-studded miniskirt I had ever seen, and she was loudly explaining to the bailiff and all who entered the courtroom that she needed protection from her husband, whom she was divorcing, and he had to stay outside at all times because of the restraining order.

You can't knit in the courtroom or drink. Or smoke. Or talk or chew gum or do anything at all but stare at the people around you and wonder what episode of daytime–talk TV they had been on. Family court is a rather unsettling experience. I suggest that if you find yourself, one day, in a situation like mine that you plan to spend the rest of the day eating an entire pie. I had already chosen one, a perfect lemon icebox pie with a graham cracker crust.

My divorce hearing could not have gone worse. And it was the pure definition of anticlimax. After all that time alone, all the money and crying and goddamn self-discovery and knitting and wine, I did not get satisfaction, or a big sum of money, or even an explanation for why he left to begin with. He didn't tell the judge about getting his creativity back, and I didn't mention the months of Cheetos and Patsy Cline. At the end of the three-hour ordeal, had the judge remanded all my cute shoes and fun memories and beloved family members into the custody of one Very-Soon-To-Be-Ex-Husband, it would not have surprised me. The sum total of my court-ordered divorce settlement was sitting at my house, probably pooping or shedding on something, and at least 25 percent of it was probably hawking up a hair ball. I got the cats, he got his freedom, and we worked out a small financial settlement on our own that cost me another million dollars for my lawyer to draw up some papers, ponder his navel, make us a stipulated something or other, add in some legal jargon, and here's your bill!

We walked out of the courtroom and said a polite and tense good-bye. All that was left to do was wait for the final papers to arrive in the mail, dissolutioning us forever.

Chapter 29

· ·

There is not enough fried chicken on the planet to soothe a broken woman.

You can eat your life into submission, or drink it down with so many bottles of wine, or smoke it away on a patio at 8:00 PM or midnight. You can look for love and respect in the eyes of another, and it still will not fill you up. This I have finally learned. Nothing will ever make you whole except you.

Not even eating a whole pie.

It is a slow process, piecing your life back together. It will not happen overnight, or over cocktails, or in three months' time. There is no expiration date on wallowing, and only the individual woman will know when her fried chicken solace has completely run out.

Being good to yourself is hard work. As women, we just do for others and hope they notice. How do you put yourself first without being seen as selfish, or mean, or miserly toward others? How do you ever move your own self to the very, absolute top of all lists?

You do it by deciding that you deserve better. Because you do deserve better.

You give yourself what you need, and you decide one day not to do it alone in your car with a drive-through bag. Or you say, "I will have one glass of wine because drinking eight-tenths of a bottle of cabernet makes my head hurt, and I want a pain-free head." You stop stuffing down your sorrow. You maybe want to eat your own head. It's okay, because the urge passes. And anyway, it is impossible to eat your own head.

When that divorce hearing was looming up on the calendar, I would lie awake in bed at night and wonder if I'd get through it. Would I just die? Die of the pain and failure and humiliation? But I didn't die, I didn't fall apart or crumble or wail miserably as he walked out of the courthouse. I felt like I didn't even know the man. He looked different, and I was already very changed, and he was just a guy I met one day. And happened to marry.

After the divorce hearing, I started taking risks. I stopped drinking wine every night because I wanted a liver that wasn't pickled with sorrow. I started small, one glass of wine followed by a fizzy water. I wasn't an alcoholic, but Lordy, I sure was trying hard to keep up with 'em. Drinking was just like eating and smoking and all of it—another way to feel numb and insulated.

Letting go of my little insulations, my coping mechanisms, was a slow process. I would eat so I didn't have to talk, drink so I didn't have to feel, smoke so I didn't have to be close to another soul. (Living in California, smokers are about as close as you can get to Satanic Spawn. In fact, Satanic Spawn will get seated faster at a restaurant than a smoker.)

Without all that self-medicating, I had to find new ways to

take care of myself. How much can I do today that makes me happy? It was a strange thing, making myself happy instead of always thinking about how to make someone else comfortable.

I had secretly hoped my whole life that if I just made people happy they would love me and need me and not leave me. I had thought if I was a good wife, my husband would have such a dependency on me that he would never leave because I completed him. I was wrong. It was good to know. It set me free a little bit each time I remembered it.

Success can be counted in the smallest things, like pouring just one-half of a glass of wine or taking a vitamin at lunchtime or going to a knitting circle. It can be that small. It can be tiny. Getting rid of all the extraneous junk collected during my marriage felt like relief. It also made my house more manageable, and I could walk to the bathroom at night without knocking over a pile of boxes and injuring a cat. Each tiny step, however small and meaningless it may have seemed at the time, was a step toward my own future. Each day that I paid a bill on time or made a dinner that did not come from a box in the freezer section felt like success.

One day I invited a coworker to lunch, and I felt victorious for simply leaving my desk and chitchatting for half an hour. On another day, a few weeks after the divorce hearing, I got up on a Saturday morning and drove to the mall where I purchased a treadmill (on a payment plan), and I moved the credenza into the garage so I could assemble that treadmill right in front of my TV. I started out slow, walking through ten minutes of the local news each morning.

Walking for ten minutes each morning felt like I was starting each day with purpose and direction. It felt like progress. It felt better than sitting alone that whole autumn and eating my problems or drinking them, and anyway, it was ten minutes.

It can be that small.

Chapter 30

. . . .

Finally winter arrived, a whole year of living in my little house. My divorce would be final any day now; I was just waiting for the paperwork to arrive. And the final legal bill, of course.

On a weekday early in December, I left my desk and walked to the elevators fully clothed for what would be my final foray that week into the cold, bleak streets of downtown Los Angeles. I was wearing the following: one winter coat; one hand-knit wool scarf; one hand-knit wool hat that did not in any way, shape, or form match the scarf; one pair of lined gloves; and one pair of insulated boots.

It was an unusually chilly evening for Los Angeles, with the temperature hovering somewhere near an unbearable forty-eight degrees. I walked onto the elevator where I saw Chris, a co-worker originally from Boston. As soon as he saw me, he began laughing at me in what can only be described as an "I am laughing *at* you, not *with* you" moment.

"It's fine," I said. "Laugh all you want. It's *cold* out there. And I get one opportunity a year to wear all the crap I knit."

"I see you took this opportunity to wear it all at one time," said Chris.

"Indeed."

He had his good hearty laugh, and then we walked off the elevators and out the main plaza doors where an icy arctic wind greeted us.

"Oh my god, it's freezing," said Chris Originally From Boston, who thinks he's much tougher than he is but yet clearly had succumbed to the prissy California weather like all good transplants.

"Yes," I said, vindicated. "It is cold for the hatless, scarfless, and gloveless. Like you. *You who scoffed.*"

"Oh my god, it's freezing," he said.

"It's so sad to see grown men shiver," I said. "You might die. It was nice knowing you."

We parted ways, and I grabbed the last express bus home. I walked in the door, set the mail on the table, and fed the cats. A fat letter from my lawyer was sitting right on top of the mail pile, mixing with the PennySaver and the weekly grocery store ads.

My divorce was final.

Chapter 31

. . . .

Christmas was fast approaching, kind of like a train, except it was one of those trains in the movies that is filled with radioactive waste and has lost all steering and braking capabilities and the conductor is boozed up and someone has a secret involving stolen money or foreign spies.

My work building was decorated for the holidays with lights on every surface, a giant tree in the lobby, and wreaths and lighted displays on every flat surface. There are fifty-two floors in this skyscraper; my company only takes up twenty-five of them, and the rest are filled with law offices, consultants, and property management groups.

A woman who works for one of the other occupants is *really*, really into Christmas. I don't know her name, but in my mind I refer to her as "Jingle." I try to avoid her, ducking into a corner or hiding behind a sparkling, well-lit ficus if I see her coming. But as luck would have it, I seem to be on the exact same elevator schedule as Jingle.

Since she doesn't work with me, I don't have to worry about her showing up at my desk, taunting me with her Holiday Superpowers, and me possibly strangling her with her own purse straps. But I do worry what I might do if we end up trapped in an elevator together. I'm not sure I can be trusted to restrain myself.

Jingle is the local Annoying Holiday Cheer Lady. She has earned her nickname because . . . she actually jingles when she walks. You may know her. You may have one in your own office or family or neighborhood, wearing Christmas appliqués and jingle-bell earrings the day after Thanksgiving. These things are fine—the bells on her socks are even kind of cheerful.

But Jingle has a dark side.

She tells you how ready she is for the holidays. She is so ready, in fact was *ready last month, last summer, last year!* She tells you how competent and perfect she is, whether you care to hear it or not. She makes you maybe want to rob a liquor store in a Santa suit.

I got trapped with Jingle in the elevator one morning about a week after my divorce was final. It was early. There were nineteen floors between me and freedom. Perhaps if I were quiet enough, she wouldn't see me. So I tried to make myself rearrange atoms and sink into the elevator on a molecular level, but I was unable to complete the metamorphosis before she accosted me.

She saw me.

She sized me up.

She pounced.

"Gooooooood morning!" jangled Jingle. "Well, you look half asleep! I just can't get enough of this great cold weather! I just love the holiday season! Don't you?"

My response sounded something like, "Whimper, whimper, sigh."

Wasting no time at all—after all, we were on a rapidly ascending elevator and time was of the essence—Jingle zeroed in for the kill.

"So, got your Christmas shopping done yet?" she asked. Smiled big.

"No?" I said. Small voice.

"Oh, my goodness," said Jingle. "You aren't one of those last-minute shoppers are you? What a headache! I got all my shopping done months ago! And I sent out all my Christmas cards last weekend, and I'm all decorated and ready to just sit back and relax!"

"I watched a John Wayne Gacy biography last night on television." I said. "He was a real clown."

Thankfully, the elevator arrived at my floor and I disembarked before talking my way into a restraining order.

I'm glad she's glad about the holidays. Really, I am. I'd just like it if she were maybe a little more silently-to-herself glad instead of aggressively glad.

The holidays are great on a conceptual level—lovely giving and sparkle lights and happy happy and family and snuggles and hot drinks with brandy or rum. Or scotch. Or vodka. Or you know, whatever. I'm flexible. But there's the fact that while I am immeasurably blessed (I am), I'm also profoundly lonely and not so twinkly, with family far away and maybe having just sent the last of my Christmas Fund off to my lawyer. There is snuggling . . . with four cats and a nice cabernet, which is . . . fine. It is!

Except . . . I am now divorced. And I am lonely.

And I suspect it is perfectly okay to be lonely. It won't kill you. It won't cripple you or give you scabies or make you unlovable. You aren't broken if you're lonely. There is no to-do list, no action item, no great sport or activity you can throw yourself into that will fill you.

Sometimes you are just lonely.

Lonely isn't a bad word, it just feels like something we *shouldn't* be, something that we must instead seek to remedy this very minute if not sooner, as if it were easy to fix, like a broken radiator or a sinus headache.

But this year I'm too tired or worn out emotionally to hide from it, and I'm just going to acknowledge it. The sad underbelly of the holidays.

I'll survive. I will not get scabies. (Because if I got scabies I guarandamntee you it would knock loneliness out of top spot for things to be sad about. Or bedbugs. Or any bugs, really. I hate them all. Bugs! The gift that keeps on giving!) And big deal, I'm lonely. It feels better to admit it.

I'm not really terrified of the holidays as much as I am terrified to get in the elevator at work because I know Jingle will be in there, and she'll be aggressively happy, and she wears a giant Christmas tree pin on her lapel that has blinking lights and plays music when you push a button . . . and I have noticed that her purse has very, very long straps.

So much better to strangle her with.

Chapter 32

• •

Christmas Eve was eighty-five degrees in Los Angeles, and sunny and perfect after a month of cold weather. I think Nature felt bad for all the times it had tried to kill me over the years, with bug bites and poison ivy and other various and sundry tools of imminent pain and danger. In an effort to make nice, it appeared Nature was giving me a Christmas that seemed more like a Fourth of July barbecue so I'd feel less maudlin and drippy about the holidays.

I decided to go to the grocery store and get some beer and other essentials before it got too late and the stores closed, or in case Nature changed its mind and gave us a tornado or earthquake.

I did not realize that every single resident of the greater Los Angeles area and their entire extended families from out of town would also be at the market. It was packed. Every shopper was in a hurry, ramming their buggies right into you. I was their worst nightmare come true, the most torturous sort of shopper—lazy and plodding in flip-flops, sunglasses on my head, tank top (!), pretending it was summer, and not the least bit in a hurry.

The main "essential" on my shopping list and the reason I had to go to the Big Grocery Store instead of my corner 7-Eleven was . . . baby food.

I do not have a baby.

I do, however, have one spoiled-rotten cat with no teeth. Roy is old, and he is 25 percent of my court-ordered divorce settlement, and I intend to keep him alive as long as possible, so as to more fully appreciate the spoils of my dissolution. With its being Christmas Eve and all, it seemed like everyone should have a little something special, including the cats. And there's nothing like a spoonful of meat pudding to make an animal happy. Until I'd started buying this delicacy for my cat, I never knew there were so many kinds of baby food! When my brothers and I were babies, my folks just mashed up whatever was for dinner and we had to like it whether we liked it or not. We liked it.

The grocery shopping experience had changed for me in the months since I'd become single again. I noticed for the very first time that there is a distinct and obvious difference between Single Groceries and Married Groceries.

Picture my groceries: Lean Cuisine, cat food, frozen burritos, salad in a bag, wine. Mrs. Married Groceries is always in line behind me. She has vegetables, or diapers, and milk and big boxes of cereal, multiple packs of snack-sized chips, family-sized jars of spaghetti sauce.

If you happen to be buying Married Groceries and shopping for your happy family of ten, please *do not comment* on someone's food when it's clear she's shopping for one plus four cats. Merely keep the witticism to yourself. The answers to all your cute questions are the following: No, I cannot cook. Yes, I have cats. Yes, I plan to eat that forty-nine-cent frozen burrito with that thirteen-dollar bottle of wine. No, I don't have time to prepare a nutritionally sound and good-looking meal . . . my twenty-two-year-old lover named . . . named . . . um? Oh! Jacques, he's from *France* you know, anyway he just tires me out so that I have no energy left over for the cooking. Why looky here, I forgot the baby oil, that just reminded me. Buh-bye!

I shuffled around the grocery store that night at a snail's pace trying to fill up a buggy with enough groceries so that it didn't look quite so painfully obvious that I would be spending the holidays alone.

I figured I may as well stock up while I was there. After half an hour of wandering the aisles, my basket contained:

Eight Lean Cuisine pizzas

Three bottles wine

One six-pack beer

One four-pack of cheap champagne in miniature bottles
   with tiny corks

Eighteen teeny jars of baby food, all meat

I stood in line behind every resident of Southern California and their uncle and flipped through a gossip magazine. Finally, I unloaded my basket, and that is when I saw the look on the checkout girl's face. She looked at my groceries, and then looked at me with nothing short of pure hatred. She *hated* me. *Hate!*

She scanned each jar of baby food individually and glared at me the whole time. I offered up a weak smile. I wanted to tell her that the baby food was for my spoiled cat, that I am not a terrible woman mistreating a child, but by doing so I would have acknowledged that she was A Judger and I was not so sure yet how I felt about needing to explain myself on Christmas Eve to a grocery store clerk. Divorce is a learn-as-you-go procedure.

Besides, it was funny. She was glaring at me like I was a drunken sot of a no-cooking, sorry-ass, baby mama. Me! A baby mama!

I could not correct her. I loved her for being mad at me for mistreating my imaginary baby. It was sweet. I wanted to hug her for being concerned for my nonexistent child's well-being. I smiled at her. She shot daggers at me. I went home and fed my damn cat his damn baby food and put the cheap champagne on to chill.

<AAmber spent that Christmas with me on the patio of my house, grilling out and enjoying the fine weather, drinking champagne out of plastic cups and gossiping about everything and nothing.

We listened to '80s music instead of Christmas songs, and lit candles on the patio table, and later we went to a movie to cap off our completely stress-free holiday. I had not finished my Christmas shopping in September (or ever), I sent zero holiday cards, I made no stuffed turkey or ham, and hung nary a light or decorative object in my entire home. I had the cats for ornamentation, and they were busily shedding everywhere to meet my high interior-decorator standards.

It was a fine Christmas, and that sadness you have about a loss fades, and loneliness eventually passes. Kind of like gas. It was also a rather *untraditional* Christmas. We grilled halibut over charcoal until it caught on fire, we laughed at each other's awesome break-dancing skills, and we vowed to bring back the leg warmers trend of 1987. Amber brought over a bottle of champagne she had customized herself by printing out a label with our pictures on it and the date, memorializing forever our holiday together. We discussed our family traditions, marriage, the merits of waxing versus shaving, and whether or not Bon Jovi would make a comeback.

It was an unconventional way to celebrate, but it was a fine, fine Christmas. And we decided not to bring back the leg warmers trend after all.

Chapter 33

· ·

After the first of the year, Jennifer and I started fantasizing endlessly about vacation. Both of us were tired and winter was dragging on, and neither of us had been on a real, bona fide vacation in years.

I love to travel. Maybe it's from moving around so much as a kid or because I lived in one small town after the next. But my whole life I wanted to travel, see the world, smell it, taste it. (I did get the tasting part down to a science.)

The last vacation I had been on was with Charlie, of course. He and I had traveled a lot together; it was my favorite time with him, and almost all our happy memories together are from vacations. When we were off on a trip together I had him all to myself with no sports on the TV, no distractions, no dinner to cook or laundry to wash or grocery shopping to do. I loved our vacations. When he left, I remember saying to Jennifer, "What will I do? I'll never get to travel again!" and I launched into a round of fierce tears.

"We'll go somewhere, you and me!" she'd said, a little cheerleader of independence. "Let's think of someplace great we want to travel . . . someplace fun, and relaxing, and . . . maybe not *too* expensive."

So we spent most of the winter trolling travel websites the way some people look at Internet pornography. I'd call her with a new find, she'd e-mail me a link to some exotic bargain, and finally we narrowed our search down to the one place I loved best and she wanted to go most: Paris, France.

I had been to Paris before, and I adored it. I loved the art and the bread and the fashionable people walking quickly off to somewhere chic, and I loved the feeling of standing in a street surrounded by buildings so old that they were practically museums on their own. Before Jen and I had started our vacation search, I would sometimes look at old pictures of vacations past and think, "Here we were on a trip to Paris and I sure look skinnier in that picture and *oh my god I will never go to Paris with him again and I am all alone and we had fun and why didn't he love me?*"

But as soon as Jennifer and I started planning and searching for flights and hotels, it all vanished, replaced by phone calls at lunchtime to discuss very important details of our upcoming vacation.

One of the main challenges was finding a hotel that both fit into our limited budgets and met the all-important shared criteria of greatness: bathtub (Jen), balcony (both of us), extremely high ratings for cleanliness (me), cheap (both of us).

With my tight budget, aggressive debt-repayment plan, and new treadmill in place, I was living paycheck to paycheck. Going on a vacation to anywhere other than my backyard seemed like an extravagance I couldn't really justify. But the more I thought about Paris, the more I thought about the need to *retake* Paris. Replace my old memories of past vacations and travel with my best friend, drink wine, and have a little fun. Take some new pictures, have new stories to tell.

Of course, traveling would cost money, and I couldn't possibly add to my credit card debt. But I was paying a hefty amount to my creditors each month as part of my antidebt moratorium. What if I just paid the minimums (plus five bucks) on each card for the next three months? That would pay for the plane ticket and the hotel, and I'd just have to be extra frugal between now and then to save up for spending money. I knew it would be a lean few months, and it probably wasn't the best and most expedient way to get out of debt. But I needed this trip.

I needed it.

Jennifer and I found a cheap flight, and we bought it. Los Angeles to Paris, round-trip! And we got such a good deal on our tickets that we called our friend Amber and told her about it, and she said, "I'm going to Paris, too!" And once Shannon heard about this girls' trip, she was already packing her perfectly matched pink bags and ready for the airport.

We were officially going on vacation! A girls' trip to Paris! What could possibly go wrong?

A cautionary word to the wise: if I am involved in your story, never ask what could possibly go wrong.

"Laurie, have you seen the news today?" It was Jennifer, calling me at work. She sounded a little wary.

"No," I said. "I've been working on this big project for my boss and I am so tired, and I tried to call in fat and sleepy, but it didn't work, and . . ."

"Okay, look online or something," she said. "I'm pretty sure it's the top headline. Paris is on fire."

"Pardon?" I must not have heard her correctly.

"They're having the worst riots in something like fifty or sixty years," she said.

"Great," I said. "Just great! I can't tell my parents I'm taking my first-ever girls' vacation to the city *of fire*. They will be all, 'I know you are an adult, but you are forbidden to go. Here, eat this piece of key lime pie instead.'"

"We might have larger issues than your parents," she said. "We might not have a hotel left."

We hung up and I scanned the Internet for news of Paris, our vacation destination to which we already had nonrefundable round-trip tickets, and it was indeed going through the worst period of violence, rioting, and civil unrest since World War II.

I phoned Jennifer.

"Okay, listen," I said. "Even if there are Apache helicopters circling the city and gangs of gun-toting youths ravaging the populace, we can take it. We're Americans, for God's sake! We get that kind of action after every college basketball game! In fact, as I say this, there are helicopters circling downtown Los Angeles, sirens are everywhere, and something is probably really on fire right down the street or maybe even in this very building, I do not know. *But we are going on vacation.*"

"Okay then!" said Jennifer. "We are going on vacation!"

We really, really needed to get away.

A few days after all four of us booked our tickets to The City Of On Fire, we began looking for a hotel to accommodate four travelers, fifty pairs of shoes, and a whole lot of luggage. We gave up the illusion of packing light very early on in the planning stages, and each of us had vowed to outdo the other on luggage size and capacity.

(Shannon won, in case you're interested. No one, and I mean *no one*, travels more well stocked than my friend Shannon.)

We finally decided on a hotel (Balcony! Bathtub! Clean and affordable!) in the charming Latin Quarter. Jennifer and I were on the phone together as I booked the rooms online and got the confirmation e-mail. We were so excited, we thought we should celebrate at my house that evening with a little wine and sit out on the back patio reading our new guidebooks.

So she came over and we sat on my patio and did a little wine tasting, then maybe a little more, and before long we decided it would be a really good idea to call the hotel we had reserved in Paris and confirm our rooms and . . . uh, chitchat. Except there were some teetiny roadblocks, like I don't know how to dial France and also, these numbers are real small, and also, maybe I should drink one more glass, and then, "Hello, France! I do not speak French!"

I believe I dialed the numbers with one eye squinted shut.

Marc at Hotel in Paris: Bonjour.

Me, drunk in the San Fernando Valley, California:
Bonjour! [Fit of giggles.] Um. Hi! Hello! Bonjour! I . . . kind
of don't know French. Whoops!

Marc: Eets okay, I speak English.

Me: [Giggle giggle.] Oooh! Yes! Hello! Thank you!

[Insert drunken conversation here about room reservations.]

Marc: Okay, everything is good, good-bye now.

Me: [Giggle giggle.] Oooh! Bonjour! Thank you!

Jennifer: [Yelling at me.] Say *merci beaucoup!*

Me: Huh?

Jennifer: [Louder.] Say *merci beaucoup!* Say it!

Me: Oh yes! Merci! Lots of Beaucoup!

After my fine job of conversing in French and confirming
the room reservations, the four of us were either staying in
side-by-side rooms with private baths at a cute hotel in Paris *or*
we were sleeping on a tablecloth covered in fleas in the back
alley. I did not know. But we had a reservation, and we were
already very familiar with French wine, and we were ready for
vacation.

I finally told my parents about our planned vacation to Paris,
even though the city was still in the middle of riots. My dad
would call me occasionally to check in and share words of wisdom about our impending trip.

"They're rioting in Paris again," he said one night on the phone.
"So I hear."

"Well," said Dad. "I have one piece of advice for you, for when
you go to France."

This ought to be a good one; I could already hear the poker
face in his voice.

"Okay, Dad. I am ready for your travel advice. Fire away."

"Don't carry any placards," he said. "All the rioters are waving
their placards."

"Thanks, Dad," I said, laughing. "I'll leave my placards at
home."

"And make sure you don't talk to any strangers. In France."

"Well, that shouldn't be a problem, Daddy, since I speak no
French!"

"You don't speak French?" he sounded surprised. "How are
you planning to order anything to eat?"

"Dad, according to your rules I'm not supposed to be talking
to strangers anyway."

"Yes, but you have to eat," he said.

"I seem to manage. . . ."

Weeks of planning, carefully selecting shoes that were both
cute and easy to walk in (not an easy task), budgeting, changing
money, finding my passport—all of it stretched out for what
seemed like an endless six weeks, and finally—finally!—our
vacation arrived.

It was a short vacation, just five days, all that we could afford. And when you are retaking a city from old memories, it's best to get in there, have some fun, and get the heck out as expediently as possible.

We landed in France on a Wednesday morning, collected our assorted three tons of baggage, and headed to the hotel. It was just as charming as the website promised, with our two rooms right across a tiny hallway from each other. Marc, the front desk attendant, remembered me from our giggly, tipsy phone call. For the next four days, we wandered Paris with maps in hand, taking photos of statues and clothes in shop windows and plates of bread. Everything we ate was covered in cheese. And wine was like water, and beer was like water, and the water was hard to find. We got serenaded by Speedy Gonzales on the metro, we got lost in Père Lachaise Cemetery, we spoke Franglish, a new language in which you mix English, broken French, and Spanish. *Très jolie!*

I could live in Paris forever; it's such a beautiful city. I carried no placards. I didn't knit once. There was no time for yarn shopping, or Internet cafés, or sticking it to the man and getting hosed with water and beaten back by police in riot gear.

The Sunday night before our short and sleep-deprived trip came to an end, the four of us walked up the Champs-Élysées and had dinner at an open-air café right on the main avenue. We watched couples walking by hand in hand, families with baby strollers, other tourists with cameras and guidebooks.

After wine and (French) fries and cheese-covered entrées, we wandered back through the city, wending our way through the streets toward the Eiffel Tower. One of the best things about being on a vacation like that is you can eat a whole city full of cheese and still walk it off in a single day. We walked for half an hour and could see the tower getting bigger. Finally, we turned a corner by a small bistro and there it was, the whole hulking mass of the Eiffel Tower looming up before us, lit from within.

Amber and Shannon decided to take the elevator up to the viewing platform, but Jennifer and I elected to stay behind, and we found a quiet bench to sit on and talk and do some people-watching.

We were chatting and resting after a long day, and fending off about three hundred trinket vendors who can be a little on the pushy side, when we saw a young couple dressed in what appeared to be promlike formal wear strolling hand in hand on the pavement beneath the tower. When they passed by us, we could hear them talking; they were Americans, too.

She had her hand in his, and when she lost her footing for just a second (high heels and a prom gown plus uneven blacktop just don't mix), he wrapped one arm around her waist and she looked up at him and smiled. And then they kissed, and I felt it deep in my bones, an ache of loneliness. I saw them smiling and laughing and enjoying Paris, perhaps wearing prom clothes but enjoying it all the same, and I felt a stab of lonely that I hadn't felt since Charlie first left.

I missed having a man put his arm around my waist. I missed holding hands, and secret smiles, and *Lord how I missed kissing.*

The young couple walked right into the middle of the open area below the glowing tower. Jennifer and I were watching them, fascinated. And before you even knew it, he was down on one knee, pulling a ring out of his pocket and she swooned and the crowd was clapping. I started clapping, too, and I started getting misty-eyed. Jennifer had by now garnered enough experience through my separation and divorce to know that misty-eyed could turn bad real quicklike.

She looked at me sideways.

"He's proposing to her in a parking lot, you freak." And we started to laugh. I'm sure she was thinking, *Good grief, do not let her start bawling over a marriage proposal at the Eiffel Tower, oh the drama!*

I sighed, caught up in the moment. I clapped some more, teary-eyed and happy, and then I turned to Jennifer, who was still watching me closely for signs of catastrophe.

I just smiled sweetly at her.

"I give it a year and a half," I said.

"Well," she laughed. "They will always have Paris!"

Later when we got back to the hotel, the other three girls decided to go out for one last Farewell-to-Vacation drink, but I said I was tired and wanted to get a jump-start on packing, and I sent them off without me. Really, I just needed a little time to myself, time to think.

I had been very surprised by my reaction at the Eiffel Tower. I hadn't felt that bone-deep longing for companionship in months and months. For so long I was holding on to Charlie, and then when I let go of that, I just held on to myself, trying the best I could to make something out of my new life as a single woman.

Part of being single again meant that I could go out and find companionship, when I was ready. And maybe I wasn't really that invested in being all alone all the time.

I stood out on the balcony and smoked my last, very last cigarette. I knew I needed to quit—it was a filthy habit. I watched as a light rain started to fall on the city. From the balcony of our hotel room you could just see the spires of Notre Dame rising up in the darkness. Somewhere a siren was going off, that wee-wah wee-wah sound from the movies, so different from America.

I guess it had been right in front of me the whole time, but I had to fly all the way to France to finally see it. It was the undeniable truth that I had neither wanted to nor hoped to acknowledge: I wanted the feel of a man's arms wrapped around me again, the warmth of a kiss, a strong arm around my waist when I stumbled in high heels and weird prom attire.

But if I were ever going to get the good hugging and male attention I needed, I would have to finally go on a real-live date.

Chapter 34

. . . .

My single friends understood my reluctance to enter the Los Angeles dating arena and didn't push me when I got back from Paris and mentioned that I was thinking about *maybe one day possibly* wanting to meet someone. *Maybe.*

My married friends? They pounced.

Married people who haven't dated in eleventy-two years love to give single women "helpful advice" about our personal lives. It's almost as if they're taking us on as an art project. I mostly find this very amusing and sweet, and I try to humor them. They're just doing it because they care. So I try to refrain from telling them how much dating has changed in a decade, and how there is now a higher chance of meeting someone who has an Internet porn addiction than meeting someone with a job. Or how much fun it is to date in Los Angeles, where your dinner companion might have served time in Pelican Bay, or run a meth lab, or be on the down low, or have four baby mamas, or be married, or—worst of all—might spend the next two hours talking about his agent, his craft, and what it means to grow as an actor. Then he'll ask you to read his screenplay.

My first fumbling steps toward real, actual dating were clumsy and more than a little embarrassing. I was still a bit wobbly in the self-esteem department, and even though I knew things had changed in the past ten years (as I reminded my married friends over and over), I had no idea *exactly* how much things had changed. Technically speaking.

I met Paul at a training seminar just as the weather was heating up, changing into summer. The whole valley was on fire from a new set of wildfires, and something about the combination of the smoke and wind and sense of ever-present danger made me a little edgy. I showed up for the class and found myself seated next to Paul, whose name I remembered because he was tall. Tall Paul.

The seminar lasted three days, and I had managed to chitchat and wear makeup and even put a fair amount of effort into my clothes. When the whole valley is on fire, it's best to be prepared with lip gloss and mascara. While it was not at all my express wish to go on a date with Paul, he was friendly enough and I was lonely enough, and Lord, if that is not a combination for failure I do not know what is. Retrospect is a cruel truth-teller. But at the time I was just happy someone was paying even a little attention to me. It felt like practicing for dating. At the end of the seminar I gave him my business card with all my contact information on it and that was that.

Until he e-mailed me a week later.

Oh, e-mail. You led me astray.

Back when I was a single girl, I used to go on dates. Like normal gals. And in this chess game we called "dating," there were rules about the telephone and when you could call or expect a call that were intricate and varied and full of loopholes. Kind of like tax law.

Being of good Southern stock, and having been schooled in the ways and means of Making Him Wait, Making Him Want More, and (of course) Making Him Think It's Over But Really You're Just Making Yourself Unattainable So He Will Want To Attain You More, I knew how to use (or not use) the telephone properly.

And then I got married, and now I am about to disclose to you a teetiny factoid that will make you realize I am old, very old, and sprouting wrinkly bits, and my ovaries are practically petrified with age: I was married *before* e-mail became a well-accepted method of interpersonal communication.

When I was a person who went on dates, there was no e-mail. And also, no Internet. They may have had the Internet in some places, maybe in cities, but I lived in the country and we had fishing nets, fishnets, and interbreeding. No *innernet.*

So the entire time I had been acquainted with electronic mail was as a Married E-mailer, and I was unaware that there were rules and also regulations in Co-ed E-mail Correspondence of the flirting variety.

At work I try to answer the 37,342 e-mails I get each day in a timely fashion. When it comes to personal e-mail correspondence, however, I always seem to be behind in the communication loop. And so in my life, e-mail has been an annoying necessity, kind of like health insurance or tampons. It has not been a way to flirt or get to know someone better.

It just never occurred to me. There was no electronic writing component of my dating years. Now, in this crazy modern world with all the technology, let's say you meet someone. You don't just swap phone numbers. *No.* You share e-mail addresses, too. And then there are some e-mail exchanges, and then you realize perhaps a little late that y'all are maybe not e-mailing just because it is the most expedient method of communication but that y'all are getting to know each other, and there are probably rules, because Lord knows men cannot handle a Woman Who E-mails Too Much (Note to self: check self-help aisle for e-mail issues books).

So you—not *me* of course—*you* call your best friend, who is younger and cuter and a better e-mailer, and your best friend schools you in E-mail Standard Time Rules & Regulations, and you listen, you do! She tells you that you have to wait a little in the response time, so a man doesn't see you as too available or needy.

But then you kind of think rules are stupid and you go off and reply straightaway, clearly sending the signal that you are a technological hootchie.

Just how on earth do people handle all the pressure to *not* respond to an e-mail immediately when it was perhaps the first e-mail all day out of all 37,342 that made you not want to staple your hand to the desk? Maybe having to wait the amount of time elapsed since he responded to your last e-mail before you can respond makes you want to staple things to your coworkers. Maybe you do not have the patience to play this stupid game.

Or maybe you have issues, and you should back slowly away from the keyboard.

Maybe.

And so I guess my permissive and rapid e-mailing sent the wrong message to Tall Paul, and he stopped writing back and I learned my lesson about E-mail Standard Time and guys. The lesson I learned was: go back to using the phone. At least that's a form of technology I am comfortable with.

As long as it isn't a real *complicated* phone.

Chapter 35

. . . .

The incident with Paul and my promiscuous e-mailing sort of started the ball rolling in the mojo department. As it turns out, mojo is not some mystical and elusive thing we can't grab on to. Mojo is just as simple as actually deciding you are finally ready to meet someone. And once you're open to it, you will.

Of course, it also helps if you are finally wearing something a little nicer than your average cat-hair-encrusted yoga pants.

The mojo can get started with just waking up to the very possibility that men are out there, and you might just be ready to meet one of them. Except there's just one teetiny catch. You may not meet exactly the man you want right out of the mojo gate. You may meet a Gary.

Gary was approximately forty years old and was a native Southern California guy. I met him at the grocery store right before the holidays—he was admiring my pears (indeed). Now I had read all those magazine articles about grocery stores being meat-markets, but I never really believed them. I suppose I was married all that time, and my grocery store visits always found me firmly on the side of Married Groceries, sending that signal out to all available dates with my family-sized jars of

Ragu, bulk boxes of Cap'n Crunch, and men's deodorant.

Yes, that's right. I once was a buyer of Married Groceries. Moving on.

Gary made some kind of fruit-related chitchat, and while I was open to mojo in general, I myself had not had any coffee yet that morning and was a little slow on the uptake. So I was surprised as anyone when Gary approached me in the parking lot as I loaded up my groceries into the Jeep.

"Hi," he said. "Remember me from the, uh, produce aisle?"

"Oh, uh, um, okay," I said. "Hi." Smooooooth as butter, that's me.

"Well, I was thinking . . . if you aren't married or have a boyfriend and you might want to get to know each other some time?" With that, he handed me his business card.

An alarm bell went off . . . business card . . . I would have to *call* him, or e-mail: Danger, Will Robinson, danger! No more e-mail!

So I sized him up, and he was normal-looking enough, and his card was from a reputable business I knew of in passing, and he had a title that didn't resemble anything such as "Murderer, Axe," and he had made all the effort to chase me out to my car, so I decided I would just write my number down and give it to him. Problem solved. And Gary called a few days later and we agreed to meet up for coffee at a little coffee shop in the Valley. No pressure. Things were going well so far, and I had not sent a single wanton e-mail.

On the evening of the pseudodate, I wore my cutest pair of jeans and reasonably girly wedge-heeled sandals, and got my hair done up, and wore lipstick and the whole nine yards. I was about quarter tilt of a full gussy-up and feeling pretty good. After all, he had chased me out to the parking lot of the grocery store, right? He must have liked something about my . . . uh, *pears*. And if I am being perfectly honest here, it had been a more-than-I-care-to-reveal long time of having no male lovin' at all in my life. I was not opposed to having some company and some non-Axe-Murdering arms circled around my waist. To get that kind of sweetness, if I had to go through this dating rigmarole then so be it.

We got our coffee and sat on the overstuffed chairs to chitchat and do the awkward get-to-know-you talking. It wasn't bad. Things were going pretty well, in fact.

Until he asked me for my exact date of birth, which was sort of odd, now that I think back on it. Most men ask for your age, or interest level in porn, or preference in barbecue sauce, or what have you, but birthday? Month and numerical day?

"Uh . . . I was born on June twenty-second," I said.

"Oh, that's too bad," said intrepid produce shopper Gary. "You're a Cancer. I'm a Leo."

I just stared at him, not really comprehending what he was trying to say. I think I must have cocked my head like a puzzled dog, because he added as an explanation, "Our signs aren't compatible."

"It was nice to meet you anyway," he said. And with that he stood up. Stood up as if he were about to *leave*.

"Um . . . ? Pardon me?" I asked. "Is something wrong?"

"I don't think we'd be a very good match," said Gary. And

with that he shook my hand (!!!), turned on his heel, and literally *fled the scene of the date.* I am not kidding. I stood right there in my little wedge sandals and my cute jeans (lover of pears, my ass!) and watched as my pseudodate practically ran to his car and peeled out like he was drag racing. I wasn't sure if "our signs aren't compatible" was the new way people told first dates they weren't interested, or if this guy really was an astrology nut, or if he'd just remembered he was married, or gay, or about to leave the country to avoid an indictment.

I looked around the now obviously very small coffee shop to see if anyone had heard this embarrassing blow-off. Perhaps I had hallucinated the whole thing. Perhaps I was just having a really bad dream, and I would look down and see I was wearing nothing but my socks, and then the alarm bell would go off and all would be well and my date with Gary, astrologer and produce aisle maven, would have been a complete figment of my warped imagination.

A woman two tables over was shaking her head and looking right at me. When my eyes met hers, she gave me a thin smile full of understanding and pity.

I had not hallucinated.

My coffee and my jeans and I went home, and it was weeks before I went on a real, real, *real* date.

Chapter 36

. . . .

Robert was thirty-eight years old and worked at the local hardware store. He had seen me in a hundred states of disarray in the past year since I was often at the hardware store purchasing supplies for projects I dreamed up in the middle of the night. He had helped me pick out the big cardboard tube that I used for my knitted cat tunnel project. He'd seen me through three furnace filters, two extension cords, a hammer, duct tape, and assorted household repairs, for I was always and forever breaking things.

I would stand there in the store, in rumpled jeans or track pants with a fine layer of cat hair, and explain my latest greatest idea while he helped me puzzle out the ingredients I might need to make each project a success.

He was a patient man. And not half-bad on the eyes, I might add.

So when he asked me out to dinner, I said yes. He arranged to pick me up at 7:00 PM the next evening and I almost lost the ability to breathe, momentarily. I was fully unprepared for *real* dating.

Dating is terrifying, really. I can list a whole host of horrible things I would rather do than go on a date, for example: try on bikinis under fluorescent lighting, get a tooth pulled, or get hairs plucked off my body one by one. Which by the way, is part of dating. There is shaving and exfoliating and prep work, and men just have no idea the full extent of the effort we put into the average date. But the first date after the Grapes of Wrath of Dating? You want it to be perfect. You want it to Go Well, and also, Not Make You Cry. You suspect that at any moment you could topple over from your precarious perch of holding-it-together and end up spilled out, guts and all, and not like that's a lot of pressure for a first date or anything.

It had not exactly started out very well from the get-go. The whole "Robert asked me to dinner" thing isn't totally, exactly, perfectly true. Robert *did* ask me out on a date *eventually,* but I have to admit that it was I who foisted my phone number upon him, in the most ungracious and unladylike of manners.

It was to this day one of the most uncomfortable moments of my life.

I am not a person who foists herself on others. I do not even foist when foisting is desired, say, with the cute UPS guy or the gardener or the checkout eye candy at Trader Joe's. I am not a foister. But apparently the filtering mechanism in my brain that keeps me from foisting was haywired by the closeness and proximity of a man who was, let's face it, smelling very, very nice and offering to help me fix something in a rather manly yet good-smelling way.

We were standing together in the aforementioned hardware store in the lumber aisle, while Robert was painstakingly measuring each plank for my new raised-bed gardening experiment. He was quite precise. I had taken a more detailed interest in this project, as you might imagine, and I was wearing a V-neck sweater and far too much perfume this time around. I hoped it masked the stench of my nervousness.

He spent twenty minutes measuring, marking, cutting each board so carefully you would have sworn he was creating art via two-by-four. After he had meticulously cut each plank to my desired length, he asked me how I planned on joining them all together to make a box.

"Uh, with nails?" I said. Convincingly, I'm sure.

"You might want to use wood screws instead," he offered. He must have seen the look on my face, another in a long line of "What have I gotten myself into?" looks, and he offered to put the boxes together in halves, so all I would need to do was take them home and join two halves together like Legos.

"I'll even make marks on the wood so you know where to put the wood screws," he offered.

I maybe swooned. A little. I resisted the urge to say, "You just said *screw*."

Thank God for small miracles.

He worked diligently on my little project for the next twenty minutes, and I stood aside and admired his way with an electric drill, and also his quite lovely and well-defined arms. As an outside observer, of course. Clearly, anyone would like those arms.

And the way he smelled.

And clearly anyone would really, really want to think about those arms a little more. In private.

Robert completed putting each box together in halves, and carefully explained to me how to join the halves when I arrived home. This way, the big boxes were in maneuverable halves and small enough so they'd fit in my Jeep. That Robert. Always thinking ahead.

Except maybe not thinking ahead to the part where I awkwardly accosted him, out of thankfulness and niceness, and commenced with the aforementioned foisting.

"Um," I said. An excellent beginning to the seduction. "Uh? I don't know how to thank you, I mean, this is so nice of you!"

"Oh," he said, "well, I'm happy to help."

"I guess, you know, I mean . . . " Wow. This was going really well. "I just want to thank you for helping me out and taking so much time to help me and everything. . . . "

"Okay," he said. "You're welcome."

Shit. Shitshit*shit.*

"Uh, well . . . ," I said, at this point I realized I was not only shaking a bit in nervousness, but I was also sweating profusely under one arm, which hopefully he could not see. "If you wanted sometime, I could . . . uh. Make you dinner? I mean, as a thank-you? Also, you can totally say no thanks right now, I mean, this is so awkward!"

And with that suave and silky invitation, how could he say no? And he replied by saying, "Oh."

That was his response.

Let me repeat it for you: "Oh."

But at this point I had come far enough along in the Humiliate Myself Triathlon that I decided it was too late to bow out gracefully. I reached right into my handbag as if I were the most confident woman on the planet, grabbed a pen and a piece of paper (old receipt from the gas station), and wrote my name and cell phone number on the back. I handed it to him.

"Here's my cell phone number, if you . . . you know. Want to have dinner. Thankssomuch seeyabye!"

And I fled. I fled the scene of the Oh My God I Foisted My Number Upon Him hardware store. They have an excellent lumber department.

I was humiliated, and sweaty under one armpit, and also . . . did I mention humiliated? What sort of cat-herding divorcee spinster *foists* her number upon the hardware store guy? I kept on berating myself in this manner for the next five minutes as I drove out of the parking lot and back toward my house, half-constructed boxes poking out the passenger side window of my Jeep.

I was so flustered I accidentally drove through a stop sign and had to slam on my brakes, much to the honking and finger-gesturing disapproval of a fellow Los Angeleno driver (hateful people who do not realize I just did some awkward foisting and am slightly rattled and perhaps not driving as professionally as usual! Stop honking, dammit!), and that is when I heard my cellular phone make the weirdest noise.

I picked it up and looked at the screen.

It said: "You have 1 unread text message."

Someone sent me a text message! Who the heck was sending me a text message? What the hell is a text message?

I clicked on the button where it said "read." I was stopped at a red light, luckily, and when the text message popped up, I about had a heart attack and died.

It said: "You R very pretty & I got shy. Lets hv dinner. Robert."

I had to pull over on the side of the road because my heart was doing flip-flops in my chest. If I was right and was reading this damn fool text message properly, Robert Hardware Store had just said yes to dinner! And I R pretty!

Then I was faced with perhaps the most humiliating and perplexing dilemma I have ever faced in all of male-female relations to this point.

How the hell do you reply to a text message?

I understand that this very question ages me, makes me part of the subset of the species known as "antiquated" and also "obsolete." But I had never sent text messages to anyone. Ever. I had no need to. You see, in my world, the world of the newly divorced and also antiquated, if I needed to tell someone something I either called them or visited. Text messaging was not part of my married life, just like flirty e-mails had never been part of the game.

In other words, I was freaking clueless. And I needed to learn this text messaging *immediately.*

So, naturally, I called Jennifer. Being younger and in law school, I assumed she was more well versed in social technology.

"Jen!" I was frantic. "Oh my God I need to know how to send a text message *right this very second or else I will die.*"

"Uh, okay," she said. "Are you all right?"

"The guy from the hardware store sent me a text message and

I have to reply but I have no clue how," I said. "Also! Less questions, more answers! *Die!* Me! About to! Remember?"

"How did he get your number?" she asked, unfazed by my "I am about to tump over and die" dramatics.

"Oh God, so embarrassing, I totally forced it on him, but whatever! Text message! Said I'm pretty! Absolves embarrassment . . . if I can figure out how to reply back, that is. Hint hint."

She carefully walked me through the steps, including how you use the numbers on the phone to type out a message. I felt like I was six years old, and also somewhat mentally challenged. After all, back in the Stone Age when I was last dating, we did not text message. We did things like ask our friends to conveniently mention we were interested to the party of our obsession.

Lord, how things had changed.

With my fat fingers and limited dexterity, it took me a good ten minutes to type a message back. As I am Southern, I chose to believe this was only heightening his interest. Making him wait anxiously to see if I would reply.

Of course, the truth is I am just slow. My chubby little digits had a hard time composing the perfect message.

"Dinner sounds good. Call me tomorrow," I typed. I felt very cutting edge. I figured I should maybe go home, watch some fresh MTV like the kids these days, throw around some cool hip-hop slang to the cats, and call it a day.

"Talk to u tomorrow. Goodnight," he wrote back.

I smiled.

I was impossibly smiley.

I had a date, almost.

Chapter 37

· ·

The predate process is exhausting. Clean your house, de-fuzz the cat hair from surfaces, tidy up, declutter as needed, vacuum, and that's just the house. There's a whole cleaning and de-fuzzing of your own self that has to happen, and here is the area where perhaps I stumbled a bit on my own first dating experience. I feel that it is my female duty to pass along some hard-earned knowledge, gleaned after some rather painful trial and error of my own.

You see, if you have also experienced a long drought in the Department Of Lovin', and you're wondering what it will be like when you "get back out there" and go on your first date, let me give you a word of advice: Do not under any circumstances use hair removal cream on your sensitive parts an hour prior to your date.

It's really good advice. I should have known this, of course. But my relationship with hair removal is tricky at best.

At age nine I was lounging in a bath and shaping soap pterodactyl plates out of my shampooed hair when I noticed my mother's pink Lady Bic razor and proceeded to mow a strip of blond baby fuzz from ankle to knee. I was a walking crop circle of poor depilation. The next day, my mother saw the clogged razor full of tiny blond hairs and asked me what on earth I was thinking, a little girl like me shaving my legs.

"Don't you know shaving is something best delayed until the last possible moment? It's like . . . like . . . mopping! You don't do it because you love it! You do it because you have to!" I did not understand her womanly ways then.

I promptly forgot all about shaving until I was about eleven years old, and then I was armed with Gillette Daisy razors and men's shaving foam and a sense of purpose because I was going to wear my first-ever pair of real panty hose (called "nylons" where I lived) and little, shiny, black patent-leather shoes with the tiniest hint of a heel, and I wanted to be Grown. Ergo, I must shave my legs.

Hair removal has always been a rather fascinating subject for me, one that was unfortunately quite public in my family after I somehow involved each person in my clan—and the good kitchen pans—in a tragic depilation gone awry. This scandal of epic cookware proportions happened the summer I turned fourteen, brought on entirely by a female classmate who had told me at school about a miraculous thing called "waxing." I spent my allowance on one box of Sally Hanson hot wax, and on a sunny Saturday morning I went downstairs after breakfast, pulled out one of my mother's Revere cookware saucers, and simmered up a pot of wax. By then my immense talent for killing all things mechanical and technical was in full force, and I avoided the microwave out of sheer fear of murdering yet another new oven. My parents loved me but had their limits; microwave ovens back then were expensive, bulky major appliances, and my father informed me I would be sent to an orphanage if I ruined another one.

I simmered my wax, and I felt sure it would be a fabulous concoction that would make my legs smooth and silky for months. I drank a huge glass of chocolate milk while complimenting myself on my fortitude for having endured two solid weeks of growing out my leg hairs to the required quarter-inch length recommended on the box. I'd had to wear pants in a sweltering Southern summer for the last eight days. I had suffered for beauty. I was rather full of myself and my female sacrifice for smoothness.

After the wax had reached the desired consistency ("like flowing honey," said the box), I glopped on a spatula full of wax on the inside of my left leg, just above the ankle. I smoothed down the white cloth strip and that is when it dawned on me.

I would have to pull that strip off my leg.

Like a Band-Aid.

A ten-inch-by-three-inch Band-Aid.

The wax was hardening on my delicate leg hairs at an alarming rate and I knew something had to be done. I ran upstairs to my older brother's room where he lay asleep, sprawled across the bed in his dark, dank teenage boy cave. I shoved him awake.

"Help me, help me, it's sticking and I can't do it."

He groaned. "[Expletive], go away, [expletive, many expletives]."

"Look," I said. I was desperate. "I will pay you. Two weeks' allowance, Guy, listen! I need your help, please?" Pleading. This was new and apparently piqued his interest.

Guy looked up at me, one eye still glued shut with sleep. "What the *hell* is wrong with you?" he asked.

I whimpered and pointed to the leg, with a crust of rapidly drying wax and a large white strip of cloth hanging to my leg hair.

"Oh my God, you're a dumbass." He laughed. I whimpered, new insult added to an already alarmingly crustier injury.

Then he said, "Jeezus, sis, you have some leg hair."

"Just pull it off, Guy, okay? Pull it off!"

"It's gonna hurt." He contemplated the scene for a minute, still foggy with sleep and perplexed by the rather large density of leg hair sprouting forth on the calves of his teenaged sister. Then it seemed to dawn on him all at once.

"It's like a huge Band-Aid. And, sis, you got some hairy legs, man. This is going to be awesome. I'm so getting you back for the time you killed my sea monkeys."

"I was five and I thought they were hungry and I cannot walk around with wax stuck on my leg, help me! I told you I will give you my allowance for the next two weeks."

"Three." Man drove a hard bargain even then.

He stared at my leg and then grabbed ahold of one end of the cloth strip and yanked off the previously hot wax, now cold concrete wax, and I screamed loud enough to pull the paint off the walls and bring my parents running into Guy's room to see who was winning the war of sibling rivalry. I was crying, and after everyone heard the story of "ol' hairy dumbass and her hot wax," my mother was laughing and my father simply shook his head and said something about "sense" and "mule" and "get out of the rain" and all seemed fine until my mother went downstairs and discovered wax permanently scorched on the inside of her saucepan. *She was not pleased.* And there was hell to pay.

So went the summer of my first waxing. And forevermore hair removal became quite the topic of conversation in our household. I was always trying out new things (but never again near the good cookware), and one Christmas, in what can only be described as the apex of family hair removal experiences, my father surprised both me and my mom with our very own personal Epilady hair-removal wands.

The Epilady was an invention in the late 1980s that promised smooth, hair-free legs and freedom from shaving! It was a handheld device with a metal coil that spun around and ripped your hair out by the roots. I used mine once and about passed out from the pain. My mom soldiered on for a few weeks, but even a beauty veteran like her eventually relegated the Epilady to the garage and eventually the dumpster. But we were damn proud of my dad, a man who knew our commitment to being fuzz free and supported it at all costs.

So I should have known, what with my extensive hair removal knowledge, that using depilatory cream just hours before a big date was a really, really bad idea. And I must have in fact been brain-dead when I decided that if smoothness and long-lasting hair removal could be accomplished on my legs, why not also spread the love and joy to my underarms and also bikini line?

Now I do not know if I have mentioned at any time during this story that I have really very sensitive skin. Skin that was not so much used to the chemicals. And I perhaps misjudged the amount of time needed for such an endeavor and somehow ended up with what felt like third-degree chemical burns in the underarm and girly regions.

My first date, which had not even officially begun yet, was off to a rousing start. I prayed for a freak cold front, seeing as I was clearly unable to wear deodorant. I opted for a skirt, what with my newly smooth legs and completely irradiated bikini line. I was in pain. I was maybe hobbling. Dating had not even officially begun, and I was a train wreck.

But I was completely 100 percent stubble free.

Chapter 38

. . . .

Robert picked me up promptly at 7:00 PM and we chitchatted for a few moments in my living room while I got my handbag and keys together and tried not to wince in pain or sweat, since I was *sans deodorant.* He looked out the large picture window that opened onto the backyard.

"So, is that the raised-bed garden you tried to make?" he asked.

"Yes, well, gardening didn't exactly go as I had anticipated," I said. "I managed to get the boxes assembled, but getting anything to grow inside them has been more of a challenge."

I had hoped the cats would stay hidden for the thirty-two seconds I had a man standing in the living room, but of course they chose this very moment to become uncharacteristically interested in human beings. Roy T. Cat walked out and flopped across the living room rug right at the feet of my date.

"Oh, you have a cat," said Robert.

"Uh huh." I didn't elaborate. Divorced with one cat is fine. Divorced with four cats? Too sexy for words.

We left the house rather quickly before the other felines could become clearly visible and headed off to a nearby restaurant. Robert had remembered that I'd lived in Louisiana as a kid, and he'd selected a Creole restaurant nearby. It was a lovely gesture, thoughtful.

After we parked, we walked to the front door, and he opened it and then placed his hand very lightly on the small of my back to usher me through the door ahead of him. It was perhaps the most intimate gesture anyone had shown me in months. I almost melted on the spot, and I could feel my whole body go tense with nervousness.

I don't want to be one of those women who needs a man for my life to hold any kind of value or purpose or meaning. But Lord, it felt nice to have a man place his hand on the small of my back and usher me through a door like a lady. All at once, I remembered the things I missed most about men, having someone touch your face, run a finger along your jawline, tell you that you look nice this evening, look at you *that way*. It makes you feel sexy to the bottoms of your toes; you walk taller, something changes, people sense it in you, you feel desired.

It's not quite the same to look in the mirror at yourself and say, "Not too shabby!" or whatever your internal pep-talk sounds like. There's just nothing I can tell myself in a mirror that comes close to that moment when you're sitting at the table and you look up from the salad plate or reach for a glass of wine, and his eyes are on you and you smile, and you feel warm all over.

It's a delicious thing. I guess maybe I never want to reach a place where I don't need it, even if that makes me a simpering old romantic fool.

Robert and I sat at a table near the window and ordered drinks and looked over the menu. We talked, all the first-date stuff you dread, but it wasn't bad. Throughout dinner, I managed not to embarrass myself or say anything terribly awkward or make a horrible fool of myself. I didn't mention that I had an entire herd of cats, but I'm sure he had his secrets, too.

Midway through the meal he asked me about my divorce.

"What happened, if you don't mind my asking?"

I hadn't really prepared for this moment. I had vacuumed and cleaned the house and removed all the hair on my body, with the pain and chemical burns to prove it, and I had bought a new outfit and fixed my hair and applied makeup so carefully you'd have thought I was meeting royalty. But I had not prepared for personal questions, for this *particular* personal question.

I was quiet for a minute. Then I told him the most truthful thing I could without going into a whole sad story, a story I just, finally, didn't feel like telling anymore.

"It just didn't work out," I said.

"How do you mean?" he asked. I probably would have asked the same thing if the tables were turned.

"Sometimes," I said, "you can have two people who are both basically good folks, and it still just doesn't work out. You grow up, grow apart, I don't know. But in the end it just isn't meant to be, and it doesn't work out."

"Do you still talk to him?" It wasn't an unfair question.

"No," I said. Maybe a little too quickly.

Before long we changed the subject and talked about work and Los Angeles and all the little things you say on a first date. The food was good. I was on a date! I went to the ladies' room before we left to make sure I didn't have anything stuck in my teeth and to reapply lipstick and catch my breath because *holy crap, I was on an actual bona fide date.*

At the end of the evening he drove me home and we stood on the doorstep and I felt for all the world like I was fifteen years old again and awkward and didn't know what to do. I fumbled with my keys. Do I invite him in? Hurry inside and lock the door? Say thank you?

"Thank you for such a nice evening," I said. Default Southern politeness. I wasn't ready to invite a man inside that way. Not yet. Plus, I was irradiated from my hair removal adventure.

"You're welcome," he said. And just like that he kissed me. We stood on the patio, and he reached up and placed his hand on my cheek and kissed me.

It was a really good kiss.

No, it was a *great* kiss.

Chapter 39

. . . .

I was driving in to work, and as I turned down Hope Street, a tour bus was letting out passengers. A group of tourists crowded around the street corner facing the Disney Center, all with cameras in hand, taking pictures from every angle. Some folks were so excited they stepped out into the street and got honked at by morning commuters.

I thought, "God, I love this city! I live in a place that people come to for vacation and make it their destination, take pictures of our beautiful landmarks to show off to relatives back home." I was in an awfully good mood. Maybe it was a little residual date hangover.

Later that night, I left downtown and drove home with the windows out on my Jeep. The air was still warm, and as I drove under the four-level freeway interchange, my car was filled with the thick, sweet smell of honeysuckle. It was so unexpected. I inhaled, thankful for once that traffic was at a standstill so I could enjoy it a moment longer. It smelled like being back home in the South, where summer is soft and warm with humidity and the fireflies light up the backyard.

Robert waited three days to call me, and when he asked me

out again I said yes. I didn't ask where specifically we would be going, just smiled ear to ear and chitchatted with him on the telephone for a few minutes, and then he said he had to get back to work and he'd call me later.

A few days later he phoned to say hey and apparently arrange the details of Date Number Two. I was happy and chatty until he said, "And so, anyway, you want to go to a dance on Sunday night?"

"What kind of dance?" I asked. If he had been able to see my face, he would have watched my eyes narrow a little with suspicion. I guess he heard it in my voice.

"Just some salsa dancing," he said. "What? You don't dance?"

And it wasn't that I didn't dance, I loved to dance, but I had not in the past had the very best experiences with Mystery Date Dances.

In high school I once got invited to a Valentine's Dance and I was so excited because the invitation was extended to me by the very tall, cute, man-about-campus Brent T., who I am sure had many other fine, redeeming qualities, but I was a teenager at the time and he had a car and a driver's license. He was also very good-looking and did I mention he had a car? A Pontiac Firebird in shiny, silver gray metallic. I almost get tingles even now thinking on how much I loved the look of that car. And the idea of the look of me in that car.

I wasn't old enough to officially "date" yet (my father had proclaimed I would be allowed to date when I finally had the "good sense God gave a fence post," which by his estimation was approximately 136 years away), but because this Valentine's

Dance happened at a church, An Official House Of God, my parents decided I could go. With one caveat: there had to be another couple along with us in the car. Apparently being alone with a boy in a car was . . . problematic?

My poor parents. They totally thought I was at the movies from ages thirteen through seventeen.

I was not at the movies.

But anyway, there I was all dressed up in my fancy clothes and sprayed from head to toe with so thick a cloud of Anaïs Anaïs perfume that it permeated every room I entered, and I had my hair hot-rollered and my lips smackered and my eye shadow and Merle Norman foundation just so. I was gussied up and ready to go.

Brent showed up at my door and picked me up, looking very nice in a blazer with his khakis, and he said his hellos and good-byes to my parents, and off we went. Except . . . we walked down the driveway to his hot car, and the couple accompanying us was his parents. Mr. and Mrs. Brent T., Sr., or more specifically, *Pastor* T. and his wife.

And when we arrived at the church it was not a dance at all. Oh sure, there was someone at the piano, and I suppose there were a few children under the age of six dancing together by the punch bowl, but it was not the lights-down-low and play-me-that-slow-song-by-Journey kind of dance.

No.

It was one of those promise ceremonies where girls were pledging vows to God and everyone that they would hang on to their virginity with their Revlon Red fingernails, swearing solemnly to never shimmy out of their panties until they were totally, 100 percent married in the Lord's church. And before long someone handed me one of these papers to sign, and I believe I made a little gasping noise, because this was not at all what I expected, and I was not about to be making promises with God based on my panties and where they might be discarded at an undisclosed time in the next twenty years.

Brent and his mom and his preacher daddy stood right there, smiling, sweet as could be, talking to me about my hootchie. Uh, I mean, my virginity. They had only the best and kindest and Christian of intentions—don't get me wrong—they were lovely people. But I am not from a family where we just sit around and discuss the future tenants of my hoohah.

I did not know what to do. I was flustered. I had already promised God I would stop pinching my little brother when he annoyed me, and I had broken that one so many times I was sure the fiery flames of hell were already licking at my feet, and no way could I promise something new to God, especially something like my hoohah, without first thinking through *how long exactly* it might be before I got married. Realistically.

And they were all watching me, waiting for me to sign on the dotted line. And I started to sweat right through my crushed velvet Laura Ashley knockoff dress. I prayed. I prayed like I had never prayed before. Not for wisdom or guidance, but for lightning to strike right then and there and set something immediately on fire so we would have to exit expediently and leave the poor, burning church house.

Nothing caught fire.

I sighed.

I was on my own.

So I looked right at them with the sweetest Christian face I could muster, and I said, "Pastor T., I'll have to take this home. My daddy says I can't sign any documents without parental consent."

And they nodded and smiled, and since I was in a house of worship, let it be known I wasn't really telling a lie. My daddy did say that, except he was talking about the time I signed my own report card at school once.

And I went home and never told my dad that Brent and his mama and daddy had tried to get me to sign a deed on my cootchie for the Lord. But it was the very last Valentine's "dance" I ever attended. And from then on out I was much more discerning in the sorts of dates I accepted, especially if "dancing" was involved.

⁓

After checking out the salsa dancing place online, I agreed to go with Robert to the club (they served alcohol, and appetizers, and the website photos showed a leggy salsa dancer in a high-cut skirt, so I assumed it would be a normal sort of dance). He picked me up right on time and we had a great night, laughing and trying not to injure each other on the dance floor. When he took me home I invited him in, just for a minute. Or two.

We went out several times over the next few weeks, and it all started coming back to me, the way you get tingles of anticipation when he hasn't called and feel a single satisfied jolt when the phone rings. The way you start shopping for something cute to wear, have a little lilt in your step, walk a little taller.

I would like to tell you that dating was just the easiest and happiest thing all the time, end of story. And sometimes it was.

But sometimes I would come home after a dinner with Robert and sit alone on the patio and have a single glass of wine (somehow drinking became less of a companion, after all, especially since I quit smoking), and I would think back over our conversation, our evening. Sometimes conversation was a struggle. I guess I'd expected it to be as easy as it was with Charlie, but of course that was an unrealistic idea. When you have been married for so long you develop an intimacy based on just knowing someone, their cadence and rhythm. It would take a while to get that with someone new.

To desire someone is like a drug; it is the only way to eat less if you always eat more, or to be hungry when you're always lean, to be needy when you're the one who is never needy. And maybe I held back a little in the desire category.

I would call my girlfriends and we talked about my dates with Robert, and eventually I told Jennifer that I, A Divorcee, Finally Had A Man Kiss Her. But I was perplexed, because even though it was a great kiss and he did have those nice arms, I still wasn't sure how I felt about him, and I could tell his jury was still out on me, too. She assured me all of it was normal, just part of the process.

"Things don't always work out," she said. "In fact, a lot of the time when you're dating, things don't work out at all."

"That's entirely *not comforting* on any level," I informed her.

"They don't work until . . . well, until one day they just do,"
she said. "That's why we keep getting back out there. It's a leap
of faith you take each time you go out with someone new."

I invited Robert over for dinner one evening, even though I
was slightly uneasy at the thought of cooking for a man; it was
an awfully intimate gesture. It was a risk. *Leap of faith,* I kept
telling myself.

We had grilled Mahi steaks with three colors of bell pepper.
It was so nice, Robert cooking the zucchini in olive oil with garlic and red pepper flakes, sautéing over high heat until just soft-
ened, still crisp. He was standing there inside my kitchen, at my
stove, helping me prepare foods my ex-husband would never eat
(zucchini, garlic, fish, a wine sauce with sun-dried tomatoes and
anticipation). Robert stirred, he lit the grill for me, he turned the
Mahi steaks, he watched me whisk through a wine sauce on the
stove. He smelled so good, and I liked the way he looked at me.

Dating is harder and easier than I expected. You just do it, you
let someone in little by little and maybe they're a good fit, maybe
they aren't, but you at least get a story to tell.

And Lord, it does feel nice to have a man in your kitchen
after all.

Chapter 40

. . . .

It's only since I got divorced that I realized I'm not bad company, that my time alone is time well spent. Because in all this time alone during the past so many months of separation and divorce and knitting, I have never felt as lonely as I did during parts of my marriage.

So I worked harder to make our marriage work. I tried everything I could to change it. We moved to a new place, I lost weight, tried counseling, stopped drinking, started drinking, made our home as nice as possible, tried to be a better listener, tried what I could to fix it. Then he left anyway.

And I know there is at least one woman out there right now who is just as scared as I was, who knows what it's like to come home at night and lie in a bed next to her husband or lover and feel completely alone. There's only so many ways you can write lonely, and I have tried them all. Nothing feels worse. You can't sleep, it's 3:00 AM, you look over at him snoring on the pillow and wonder why he is so far away, an unreachable distance.

And I can also tell you that you do make it through the other end of a thing, and if your life changes and doesn't go according to plan, you make a new life for yourself, and it can be a really good life. It can be a happy life. Every night I go home to my little tiny house and my herd of cats, and the night is mine, mine to do with it what I will. Mine to invite someone into if I choose, mine to sit on the patio with a friend, mine to figure out who I am now. The scary parts are still there, but you just wade through them. And sometimes you cry, or drink nine-tenths of a bottle of cabernet, or look at old photos.

And sometimes you paint your toenails, or read a good book, or call an old friend or a new one, and sometimes you go to dinner with someone who looks at you like you're pretty, and it doesn't mean you lose yourself.

You're just finally showing up for things, truly present the best way you know how, and it can be really, really nice . . . even if it's just one moment, one small glance. You enjoy the choice. The opportunity to be yourself, whoever that is, to feel a hand around your waist, a kiss on the collarbone, not because you can't be without it but because it's so warm and inviting, because it's lovely to spend time with others when you're in your new life, the one you were never sure you'd have.

Chapter 41

. . . .

One Saturday morning about six weeks into my relationship with Robert, I got up, got dressed, drove myself to the Farmers Market in West Hollywood, and attended the once-a-month Saturday meeting of Stitch 'n Bitch. Many of the ladies in attendance were expert knitters, ranging in age from mid-thirties to well near eighty years of age. It is a nice group, a very well-behaved, polite group.

There's a reason I am mentioning that, about them being so ladylike and well brought up and all.

I walked into Stitch 'n Bitch with my knitting bag and smile, and all the ladies started to immediately look at me anew, commenting on how lovely I looked that day. Had I lost weight? Gotten my hair done? What had I done differently, they asked. I looked so great! Just glowing!

And I wanted to perch up on a table and holler loud and clear a proclamation. That I, one divorced now thirty-four-year-old woman with four cats and a penchant for the wine bottle *finally had really great sex.*

I did not make this proclamation.

But I really wanted to shout it out from the rooftop.

So when Faith finally arrived ("Wow, Laurie, you look great! Do you have on a new lipstick? You are just radiant today!"), I grabbed her by the elbow and dragged her downstairs. I had to tell someone.

"Faith. I *had sex. Sex sex sexsexsex.*"

She started laughing. She was laughing so hard she was half-bent over outside the doughnut shop.

"And, Faith, in case you were wondering, it was really good!"

"I can see that," she said. "Seriously. You needed this, apparently!"

"I had no idea," I confided. I was whispering now. "I do believe I am alive."

And we giggled, and I did perhaps a little more confiding, and we went back upstairs and the fair ladies of Stitch 'n Bitch were spared a proclamation. Amen.

❦

eAnd just like that, my light was flipped back on.

I wasn't just a woman who'd had a long, old dry spell, or a divorcee, or a cat herder. I was a woman who was vibrant and pretty and alive. It wasn't because Robert was magical, don't get me wrong. He was not magic. (That area is the sole purview of my hairdresser.) He was, however, sweet to me and I took a leap of faith to let myself feel something for someone new. I didn't pretend to be in love, and I didn't start planning a walk down the aisle, I just enjoyed his company and enjoyed the time we had together. That enjoyment and happiness leaked over into my everyday life, which is why random coworkers would stop me to ask if I had lost weight or cut my hair.

There is something about happy that is contagious and gives you the ability to see your life in unexpected ways. I wanted to grab hold of that feeling and keep it. I knew it wouldn't disappear if Robert left because I had the hope inside me. I had the pretty inside me. He had seen it, and so could others. So could I.

After my husband left I had been terrified that people wouldn't find me pleasing. Would not like me. I would feel mortally wounded when someone said an unkind thing. I hated admitting that out loud, too. I hated saying "My husband left me." I felt broken, and flawed and ugly.

But I guess somewhere along the line I felt really blessed to be stripped down so naked with just my blubbering and crying and eating Cheetos off my chest, because I couldn't keep up *any* facade, I couldn't pretend to be anything at all. I was just a heap, and I knew it, and so did the world. It was kind of a relief, being a train wreck. It was almost a comfort to just be something real, even if it was real ugly.

When I met Robert I had tentatively begun to feel out my new, true self. I had slowly started making friends, carving out a life for myself, however small and cat-infested that might be. He was kind, and we had fun, and I managed to hold on to my new self without immediately trying to conform to some picture I assumed he held of the perfect gal. I just tried to be myself. That was a new and startling concept.

Other new and startling events happened when I began

dating Robert. With the certainty of hugging and kissing and eventual nakedness back in my life, I decided I should go and buy some fancy panties. Now, I had not gone shopping for lingerie in many moons, and the new and startling part of this excursion was the sheer complexity and variety available for women of all shapes and sizes. And also what a surprising amount of things can be shaped out of black vinyl!

I browsed the aisles of the lingerie store for half an hour, picking up items on the hanger and trying to envision how exactly one might get it on her body. Would you need to know yoga? Would you need some sort of oil to get things slipping on more easily? And furthermore, how exactly do you get *out* of such a contraption?

My only experience in the past with fancy and complicated lingerie occurred in college with my longtime sweetheart. I had managed to shimmy into some lacy, frilly getup, but by the end of the evening my boyfriend had to literally *cut me out of it.* After several glasses of wine and maybe some Jell-O shooters at the local university hangout, neither of us could figure out how to get the thing off. Before long I was making funny voices and saying, "Well, I declare! She gone and died in her fancy panties! Her fancy panties up and attacked her while she was being sexy!" Of course it wasn't sexy at all by that point, but we managed somehow to laugh ourselves silly, then accidentally set something on fire when we knocked over a candle while cutting off sixty dollars of very, very complicated lingerie.

Robert was a handy guy at the hardware store, but even this might be out of his area of expertise. I didn't want to set my little

Encino house on fire or have to phone 911 for assistance with my underwear. So I selected a matching bra and pants set in a lacy and demure ivory color. While I stood in line waiting to pay for my not-very-naughty underwear, the woman in front of me plunked down two hundred dollars on something vinyl with buckles and about three hundred little grommets and a lot of red lacing.

The sales clerk wrapped up the unique and slippery-looking item, and the woman in front of me collected her bag and turned to leave. As she looked down at my virginal bra and lacy under-wear—not even a thong—I quaked for just a minute, wondering if I were somehow lacking in the naughty department, failing at this new and more complex world of dating, again, missing out on some critical knowledge about vinyl.

But then I just smiled, stood up straight, and she smiled back.

To each their own.

Chapter 42

· ·

All good endeavors in life require a list, and dating is no different.

That first date with Robert was fabulous. The second date was fabulous, even if I did end up with two bruised toes from salsa dancing gone wrong. All of our time together unfolded with fewer hiccups than I expected. We didn't work out as a couple in the end; Robert was anxious to leave the hardware store and find a job out in the ocean somewhere as a diver and underwater welder, and I wasn't looking for a long-term all-encompassing relationship again. I believe they call this a "rebound."

But Lord, those first few weeks were exhilarating, like skydiving in your cute shoes, and you feel pretty all the time and want more, more, more.

He would take me out on dates or I cooked dinner for him, and when he walked up behind me in the kitchen one evening and wrapped his arms around me, I felt like I had suddenly gotten an infusion of Diet Coke times ten, warm and electric at the same time. It was the same when he kissed me the very first time, and all of a sudden I realized how good a man could smell and feel all at once. It was like being awake again, where you're pretty sure you feel each nerve ending wake up from hibernation, and my don't you look good today!

So dating isn't all bad. You just need a list.

You need a list of what you will and will not put up with. How you want to be treated. What you need and want from a person. What you are willing to give. (Also, a questionnaire for prospective dates is not a bad idea. Maybe with character references and legal history.) A date gone wrong can make you want to sit in a corner and eat your own head. A date gone right can make you feel skinnier and giddy and rather full of yourself.

The key is to know you deserve the superdates, the ones that make you feel fabulous. I guess if I'm honest I've just been experimenting, trying to figure it out as I go, not sure exactly how much I can demand from a man or from anyone really. What are we worth? What can we reasonably expect from people? What do we deserve?

I suspect a lot of people wonder this. Where do I set the bar? Not too high so as to exclude good men, but not too low so as to find me sitting in a corner exasperated and contemplating eating my own head on a Saturday night?

When I was fourteen and awkward and in love with my hair, I got a new curling iron with my allowance. After school one day I made my mom sit on the closed toilet seat (blue carpet fuzzy cover, I remember that one for sure), while I curled her hair just so, trying out my new implement of beauty.

She was patient, even though I am sure I was not the most delicate of hair stylists. Around 5:00 PM she heard the downstairs garage door open, and got antsy real quicklike.

"Hurry, finish up!" she said.

"But I'm not DONE YET," I said. Beauty was an art, you know.

"Your dad is home; I want to see him when he walks in," she said.

It was a mystery to me. Who cared? Dad got home every day. I only got a new curling iron once a millennium.

But I saw her squirming, ready to bolt from my bathroom beauty salon, and I realized then—at fourteen years old—she was so slaphappy to see my dad she was about to keel over. I didn't know it at the moment, but this would become exactly my yardstick one day for who I would let into my life.

Because I want that! I want to feel squirmy and happy and just pleased to see the look of a person. I don't need another marriage, another promise, another ring. I just need a real warmth, some good laughing and loving, someone who can adore me in the manner to which I would like to become accustomed. And hopefully he likes cats.

It's a good thing to make a list, figure out what you want, and know what you are worth. Dating is hard, and sometimes it's boring, or awful, or slow. Sometimes it gives you a story to tell, and not all these stories are of the heartwarming variety. It can be hard to meet people. It may feel easier to settle than to keep on keeping on. Whether that is settling for being alone or just settling for less, or more of the same, it's all driven out of fear. And trust me, I know fear.

Each of us deserves kindness, honesty, something fun and

warm and happy that makes us feel alive down to our very toes. We all deserve a little slice of happy. Even those of us who sometimes want to give up, or complain a lot, or hide under the covers out of exhaustion. And it's not all bad. Sometimes you have a hand on the small of your back or a really good kiss or a warm evening when you think maybe, just maybe, I can really do this. Maybe.

*After a few months Robert told me he'd been offered a job doing underwater welding offshore. He was ready to go off and resume his life as a diver, and in the end we parted on good terms, and I was proud of that. Robert may never know what he meant to me, that he gave me a little glimpse into my future, that when he placed a cupped hand on my cheek or told me he liked my laugh, it brought me joy and restored my faith in men.

It didn't make me sad that he was leaving, because I knew if God made one good man with nice arms and a sweet disposition, he must have made a few more along with him. Robert was proof that good guys were out there, and good-looking ones, and I do not regret one moment of that relationship.

I also have some very nice lingerie now.

Just in case.

Chapter 43

Commuting takes up so much of my time, yet secretly there are nights when I'm completely happy to be a prisoner of the express bus, suspended between the demands of work and the responsibilities of my house. It releases you of all pressure to make phone calls, finish e-mails, send updates to presentations. You just sit on the bus. There are no dishes that can be washed, or laundry that can be done, or cats that can be fed. You can listen to music, or knit, or read a magazine, or do absolutely blissful nothing.

My favorite nights are when the bus driver turns off the overhead fluorescent lights and everyone is silent; some people are sleeping, and the bus is dark, and you can look out at the cars going by, totally enveloped in quiet suspension. All you hear is the soothing drone of the bus motor.

On those nights I just look out the window and think. Sometimes I re-say conversations I wish I'd handled better, or I daydream about vacation, or plan things for the future, imagining who I might be one day or where I might live. Sometimes I think about the past. I pinpoint the things I did wrong in my marriage, analyze ways to improve, make a Not-To-Do list in my head.

It's not what you think. I'm not berating myself, or blaming myself, or fantasizing that it would end another way, or not end at all. I'm not hoping to sprout time-travel wings and go backward. The past is behind me, and I don't want to change it. I do not want that marriage back.

But I need to feel like an active participant in my own life, a part of the success or failure of a thing; I need to know how I contributed one way or another so I can be better, happier, stronger, kinder.

My list is a good one: Have more sex. Hire a cleaning service so you spend less time being resentful. Go out on dates at least once a week. Always be kind, even when you want to be mean. Listen more, talk less. Don't drink too much wine at a party and accuse him of . . . anything. Wear sexier stuff to bed. Have your own life. Have your own goals, interests, and activities. Don't give up being whole. Don't pick someone who'd need you to be less than you are. Choose well. Don't criticize his driving.

This is the optimist inside me thinking that if I can improve, learn from my past mistakes, perhaps I will have a better future. Maybe it's my control enthusiast side coming out.

~⟡~

After a long week of working and commuting and paying the bills and generally passing as an adult, I will sometimes re-tool the budget just a little to find just a tiny bit extra as a reward. One evening I caught an early bus home and drove myself to a shoe store for just the reward I'd been waiting for.

I was standing in the aisle and gazing at five different kinds of black boots when it dawned on me: *You get to choose.*

You get to choose everything, now, from which boots you want (wear the high-high heel and not care if you tower over a man) to how long to wallow in sadness, how much of your self-esteem to let go of.

Who says shopping isn't therapeutic?

I chose knitting even though it seemed like a mighty strange activity at the time. Some people would have exercised or gone to a bar, and that's their choice. I selected wool and merino blends and soft, lush cashmere when I needed to splurge. When I went to get my hair cut, I picked out a strawberry blonde highlight color because I needed a change, and if we weren't going with bangs, we were going *red.*

At some point, you have to choose. You can't forever be a victim, held prisoner by your own crying. You cry it out.

I stood there looking at the shoes and thinking all these crazy thoughts. On the other side of divorce was a whole new life. The life where I colored my hair any old color I wanted and never thought twice about anyone's opinion of it. I had a choice: either stay right there in the sad but comfortably worn spot on the sofa or throw my cards in with the unknown. I had no idea what was coming next. It might be worse, worse than lonely. I immediately wanted to run home, abandon shoe shopping, revert back to the smallest and safest place possible.

I ran my index finger down the center seam of a buttery smooth black leather boot. When was the last time I wore something so beautiful?

And when had I decided that it always had to be something bad around the next bend? Whatever was coming next might also be very, very good. Luck is fifty-fifty, right? And if good luck can run out, then maybe bad luck can run out, too. Maybe a woman can decide that she's going to come out the other side of this thing and she is better for it. Stronger. Happier. Alive.

I bought the highest-heeled black boot they had. Whatever was coming, I wanted to be properly prepared for it, from a footwear perspective.

Chapter 44

. . . .

Even with the addition of not just one or two but five new pairs of shoes, my little house was growing cleaner and less clutter free each month. My garage, however, was becoming a scary and disorganized mess. My system of paring down had worked really well for me: Put a bag or empty box in a corner of my kitchen and inside each closet to catch clutter. Whenever I'd run across some object that was no longer needed or useful—into the bag or box it would go. After the container filled up, I hauled it out to the garage for some future yard sale, date unknown.

When I could no longer walk in the garage and the clutter began to creep over to the washer and dryer, I decided it was finally time to have the end-all be-all Purge Marathon Yard Sale. Faith enthusiastically offered to help me. (She is much better at the concept of yard "sale" than I am, as I tend to wither under scrutiny of bargaining—Southern folks do not want to haggle; we would like to bring you a nice casserole instead.) Faith and her husband live in a house so tidy you just feel a Zen calm wash over you the minute you walk in.

We decided on a day for the big yard sale, and I made huge, bright signs on poster board while she got busy placing ads online and in local newspapers. I came home from work each night energized to pare down! Be clutter free! And I walked through my little house looking inside cupboards and closets for hidden junk, clothes I would never fit into again, old cowboy boots I was too afraid to try on for fear a spider had taken up residence in the toe. Let some stranger buy those boots and the spider family inside—one dollar, please!

When I had moved into this house I hadn't been willing to get rid of a single thing, as if holding on to objects could somehow save enough of my old life to be resurrected, marriage and all. After a few weeks of living in this little firetrap, I knew it was a physical necessity to pare down (I kept losing track of my keys, my cats, my shoes), so I got rid of what I could.

But for a long time I still held on to pieces. I just had no idea what to replace them with, and I was too scared of being empty.

Now, I wanted a different coffee table than the one Charlie and I had picked up at a thrift store, a different desk than the one Charlie and I had shared. And for new desks and tables and happy moments to come into my life, there had to be room. As long as that wobbly, banged-up coffee table occupied the middle of my living room, a new one couldn't show up. I had to make space for a new life to take root.

That is when I made my big proclamation. I often get myself in trouble with late-night proclamations made after too little sleep and too much wine. I believe one evening, in an ill-fated attempt to make my personal fashion sense a little more cutting-edge, I vowed—nay, *proclaimed*—to bring back the side ponytail. Luckily on that particular evening I was with a group of girls who had also lived through 1980s fashion like I had, and they all laughed and I got to pretend my solid declaration was just a little tipsy joke.

But as I looked around the living room for more items to add to the growing yard-sale pile, I declared aloud to all four cats and As God Is My Witness that any object that started with "Charlie and I . . . " had to go. If the sole memory I had of a thing was "Charlie and I bought that on vacation . . ." or "Charlie gave that to me as a gift . . . ," then it was time for it to leave and find a new home. Good riddance and say hey to your mama.

The night before your big yard sale that you have no idea how to pull off because you have never actually hosted a yard sale before, you should definitely do the following:

• Get sleep

• Get organized

• Perform productive yard sale preparation tasks

I did none of those things. I instead chatted on the phone with my parents, painted my toenails, and cut pictures of perfect future desks out of the Pottery Barn catalog.

The Saturday morning of Garage Sale Day arrived. I had not even hung the first sign and already people were flocking to my house. Darn early birds!

Now, it is true that I myself tend to wake up at the first buttcrack of dawn and yes, I may be at the 7-Eleven at 5:30 in the morning for a newspaper, or perhaps I'll do a little grocery shopping at 6:00 AM, because I am an insomniac, and also, crazy, but Good Lord in Heaven, you will not find me pulling my car up into someone's driveway with such a fervor that I almost drive onto the yard itself, snatching clothes left and right, haggling, all before anything is even totally set up. No matter how much of a morning person I might be, it would never cross my mind to show up at your house at 6:20 AM looking for a coffee table bargain! And be rude to you! And also, steal things off your lawn!

Yes. I said *stealing*.

Is this a new thing or is this part of sale-ing the yard? Jennifer and Faith and I stood there in fascinated horror as a vanload of women shoved our yard sale clothing into their handbags. And then drove off with their heads held high, like nothing in our yard sale had appealed to them thankyouverymuch. A man walked off with my Fossil watch. Jen's pajama pants disappeared. (She wasn't wearing them, in case you were wondering. Just for clarity's sake.)

Initially, I decided that if you were having bad enough times that you had to steal from a yard sale, well, then you should take it. Just take it! Please! I would have donated it to Goodwill anyway, and probably should have 'cause all the misbehavior happening on the front lawn before 7:00 AM was freaking out my poor, caffeine-deprived brain.

But then I started thinking about it a little. Cogitating. When I was little we were poor. We were so poor in fact that we were just plain *po*. But stealing? That was never an option, and especially not off someone's front yard. I'm just saying, is all.

Finally, we dispatched a neighbor to watch the front lawn, Jennifer took patrol of the sidewalk, and Faith stood her ground over on the driveway. While folks meandered through piles of clothes and assorted mismatched furniture (How did I manage to fit four occasional tables inside my tiny house?), I was still hauling stuff out of the garage, box after box after box after bag.

"My goodness," said one early birder. She had been watching me bring loads of crap out of the depths of the garage for a good fifteen minutes. "You have so much stuff! Is there even anything left in the house? Are you moving? *Is it empty?*"

I stood stock-still for just a moment and looked out on the driveway, the yard, the whole sidewalk—all covered in stuff. The exposed bags and boxes of junk-store clutter were a big old sorry piled-up testament to the pain of my unhappy marriage, all the times I had shopped to make myself feel better even if all I could afford were discount bins or thrift stores. I shopped. I bought to fill up the empty. I shopped and shopped and shopped and hoped for a better life, to finally feel fulfilled, to be whole and surrounded.

Each and every thing on display that day was a testament to my loneliness back then. How is it that a married woman can feel so much lonelier than a single woman? Sure, I'd had long nights of aloneness and seclusion as a separated and newly divorced woman, but my single life now was more warm and crowded with love than I had ever felt back then, back when.

The manic crowd of yard sale snatchers faded as the morning wore on. The stealing hordes only came for the first hour; I guess they count on you to be half-asleep and still busy setting up. After that it was nice folks stopping by, just normal people and families out for a day, doing some neighborhood shopping. And

I got to chitchat with all kinds of folks, and practice my Spanish, and make an ass out of myself asking everyone if we had the best yard sale signs they had ever seen. (Seriously though? Our signs kicked every other yard sale's butt! I was sure of it.)

Later in the morning some girlfriends I had met through my knitting group arrived and someone brought blessed coffee, and two of the gals brought their babies to sit on the lawn and crawl across piles of assorted clothing.

I had found people to be surrounded by, somehow, in my good luck. People, not junk! When the afternoon came and the customers dwindled, all of us girls sat out on the blankets spread on the front lawn and chitchatted, looked at the shrinking piles of stuff, and speculated on how much money I had made.

I looked at them and thought, *I love my friends, I love not needing to buy something to make me feel worthwhile anymore!*

A few of the girls who stopped by that day had never been to my house before, and I was so relieved to be able to invite them inside. I could actually show them around my house and they weren't eclipsed by junk. When I gave them the grand tour of my spacious eight-hundred-square-foot house, it actually *felt* spacious! There were no teetering piles of stuff in the corner, no clutter to step over, no rooms that had to be explained away with a quick closing of the door. Instead of feeling sad or empty to let go of all that stuff, I just felt free!

Midway through the yard sale, an older gentleman pointed at an object I had pulled out of the garage but hadn't fully unpacked from the box.

"What is that? A VCR?" he asked.

"Oh, that is a DVD player," I said. "It's just like new! You can have it for only five bucks, too. It was my ex-husband's."

"I'll take it," he said. "Say, you got anything else of your ex-husband's lying around you want to sell to me?"

"Well, there was a picture of me and him around here somewhere," I said, laughing. "It's yours for free if you can find it."

And I am proud to tell you that later in the afternoon I made a dollar selling someone that very frame containing a photo of me and one ex-husband. I hadn't really intended to put that picture out for sale, but it was one of those complicated frames that required a screwdriver and a degree from MIT to unhinge, and finally one evening months before the yard sale, I gave up trying to dislodge the back panel and threw the whole thing into the sale pile. I had forgotten about it until that very morning, when I saw Faith had arranged all the picture frames and knick-knacks on a table for maximum retail impact, and there was the picture of me and Charlie right smack in the middle.

A woman browsing around the knickknacks had her arms full of picture frames.

"If you're looking for a mighty pretty frame, I got just the one for you," I told her. "That's me and my ex-husband in the picture."

She looked at me for a minute, then, all of a sudden was more curious about the weirdo gal with the growing sunburn and twangy accent.

"You should take him right off my hands," I told her. "One dollar, bargain at any price!"

And she bought it!

My friends and I waited until she left before we started howling with laughter. We must have joked about that picture frame for hours and retold the story to everyone new who showed up that day.

Yes, I wanted good things to come into my life. Good people. More laughing.

Now I had space for them.

⁘

𝒯he yard sale is over, I'm sunburned and tired but I am four hundred dollars richer and a lifetime lighter.

It's late and I'm sitting on the porch, out back, in a faded wicker chair whose cushion has seen better days. It's still warm out; I can hear the crickets talking to each other.

I have on pajama pants, wrinkled and soft; there's a hole in the left leg where I got caught on the bushes once on my way to the garage before Francisco the gardener cut the shrubs down to a stump. Everything is quiet, except the crickets and occasionally a plane overhead to remind me I'm in Los Angeles; I'm in a city of millions and being alone is a luxury, or chance, or just the way it is right now.

I've poured myself a glass of wine and stretched out to relax and think about what sort of new coffee table I might want and fantasize a little about new pictures in new frames that might decorate my house one day.

A good cabernet, and four hundred dollars from old junk . . . not too shabby for a Saturday afternoon, if I do say so myself! I will drink coffee in bed tomorrow, and treat myself to a pedicure, and clean the cat box, and probably need to go purchase some aloe vera gel for this sunburn.

I stretch and feel muscles I haven't used in a while, hauling out all that old furniture and clutter. But it's a good ache, the bone-tired feeling of a job well done, a day well spent. Parts of me are like this very cushion I'm sitting on and have seen better days, but parts of me know there are so many better days to come. There will be new adventures and interesting shoes and good-looking men and fine afternoons with friends, and I might even learn to make a sweater one day instead of just hats and scarves. I wonder if I can knit a picture frame? I bet there is a pattern out there somewhere for it.

Had Charlie stayed, I may never have taken up knitting. And had I not become obsessed with knitting and yarn and writing it all down, I would not have met Ellen, who wouldn't have invited me to a Stitch 'n Bitch, and I wouldn't have met all the West Hollywood knitters, some of whom are now my dearest friends.

Had Charlie stayed, I may never have had the guts to face my finances and save up for a trip to Paris with my girlfriends, and so I would never have seen those two people kissing so passionately under the Eiffel Tower and wished for one more chance at real love. Which would have meant I'd never gone out on that first date, and I would have missed out on some pretty great kissing and one or five funny stories. My life might have stayed cluttered up with old junk.

Had Charlie stayed, I might have never figured out what kind of woman I am.

I used to think that the day he left was where my story began, but maybe this is where the story really gets going.

It's crazy, I tell you, the way life works out.

Knitting Recipes

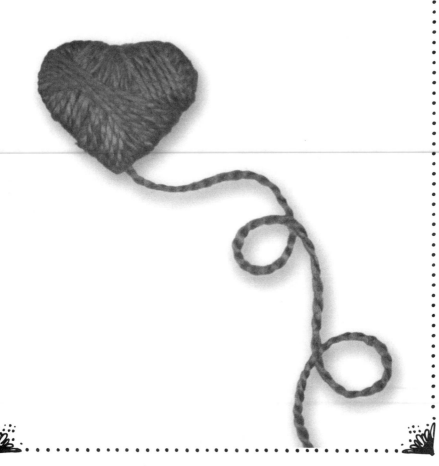

KNITTING TERMINOLOGY 101:

Some of the patterns (mostly, the ones written by me) are like little stories on their own, as I prefer patterns not to have too many confusing abbreviations, especially when there is wine involved in my knitting! However, normal pattern-makers create all their knitted treasures using crafty shorthand. Here is a brief key to the abbreviations you may see used in the following knitting patterns.

beg = beginning

BO = bind off

CC = contrasting color

CO = cast on

C6F = Cable 6 front (cable 6 stitches to the front);

C6L = Cable 6 left (cable 6 stitches with left twist);

dec = decrease

dpn = double-pointed needles

ea = each

g = gram

inc = increase

incl = inclusive

K = knit

kfb = knit into the front and the back of the stitch (as in an M1)

K1 (2, 3, etc.) = knit 1 (2, 3, etc.) stitch(es)

K1b or **K1-b** = knit one stitch through back loop

k2tog, or **k2togR** = knit 2 stitches together

Kwise or **K-wise** = knitwise, as though to knit

LH = left hand

M1 (2, 3, etc.) = make 1 (2, 3, etc.) stitch(es)

MC = main color

oz = ounce

P = purl

patt. = pattern

P1b or **P1-b** = purl one through back loop

PM = place marker

psso = pass slipped stitch over

p2sso = pass 2 slipped stitches over

P2tog = purl two stitches together

Pwise or **P-wise** = Purlwise, or as though to purl

rem = remaining

rep, or Rep = repeat

RH = right hand

rib = ribbing

RS = right side

sc = single crochet

SKP = slip 1 stitch, knit 1 stitch, pass the slipped stitch over the knit st

SK2P = slip one stitch, knit next two stitches together, pass slipped stitch over the k2tog, 2 stitches decreased

sl = slip one stitch

sl-K = slip stitch knitwise

sl-P = slip 1 stitch purlwise

ssk = slip stitch knit (slip, slip, knit the 2 slipped stitches together)

St = stockinette st (knit 1 row, purl 1 row)

sts = stitches

tbl = through back loop

tog = together

WS = wrong side

wyib = with yarn in back

wyif = with yarn in front

The Basic Beginner Scarf

Every beginner starts off with a plain old garter stitch scarf, casting on and knitting every stitch of every row. I think simple garter stitch scarves can be so beautiful! With a gorgeous yarn, the lowly garter stitch is elevated to something classic and graceful.

INGREDIENTS:

- **Yarn**: 1 skein Noro Transitions. A very expensive and beautiful yarn, it not only changes colors, magically creating a self-striping scarf, this yarn also changes fiber. From silk to cashmere to camel to who knows what.
- **Needles**: Size 11 needles

THE RECIPE:

Cast on 18 stitches and knit every row for a soft, airy, beautiful scarf.

 Beginner Scarf #2

INGREDIENTS:

♦ **Yarn:** 1 skein Rowan cotton tape or any "tape" or ribbon-style yarn. Using a ribbon-style yarn on a garter stitch scarf makes an elegant fabric, and most ribbon and tape yarns are smooth and easy enough for any beginner.

♦ **Needles:** Size 10 needles

THE RECIPE:

Cast on 15 stitches and knit every row.

The most important thing to remember with your first scarf is to select a yarn you LOVE. As long as you love the color and texture of your yarn, you'll be happy with the finished piece.

❧ Magic Scarf ❧

The concept behind this scarf is so cool. You make little blocks of stock-inette stitch. Some blocks are stockinette, and some are reverse stock-inette; together they make a checkerboard!

INGREDIENTS:

♦ **Yarn**: I used Noro Kureyon, but this pattern will work for any worsted-weight yarn. One skein will make a lovely scarf; two skeins make an extra-long beauty.

♦ **Needles**: For the Noro, I used size 10.5 needles.

♦ **Wine Selection**: A hearty Shiraz

♦ **Accessories**: Row/stitch counter, if you have one handy

THE RECIPE:

Step 1: Cast on 20 stitches.

Step 2: Knit 5 stitches. Purl 5. Knit 5. Purl 5. Repeat for ten rows.

Step 3: Magic time! On row 11, begin the row with purl 5, then knit 5, purl 5, knit 5.

Repeat for ten rows.

Step 4: On row 21, return to knit 5, purl 5. Simply knit 5, purl 5 for ten rows. On and on and on. I did this for nine feet. I am crazy.

Step 5: Bind off. Love. Enjoy!

Can it get any easier?

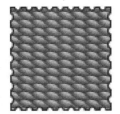

Reverse stockinette
bumps all on
one side

Stockinette smooth & pretty
(use your imagination
on the illustration)

① Begin knitting a row. Knit 5 stitches then purl 5, knit 5, purl 5. First row complete.

| knits | purls | knits | purls |

② When you flip the needles around and start knitting the next row, you're just repeating the same old knit 5, purl 5, but now you have:

| knits | purls | knits | purls |
| sllnd | stiuʞ | sllnd | stiuʞ |

· ·

Knit ten rows: knit 5, purl 5, knit 5, purl 5.
Then knit ten rows: purl 5, knit 5, purl 5, knit 5.

Knit	Purl	Knit	Purl

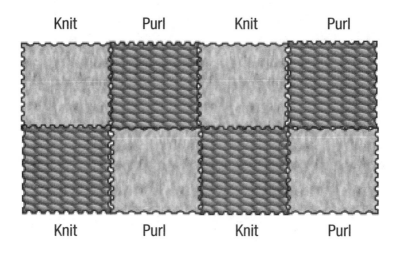

Knit	Purl	Knit	Purl

ALTERATIONS TO THE RECIPE:

Knit three rows of garter stitch at the beginning and end of the scarf to keep it nice and flat.

Knit 3 stitches of garter stitch on the edges.

Add fringe: Cut yarn into 12 inch-long strands. Hold about five strands together and fold them in half (more strands make a denser fringe). Use a crochet hook to draw the center of the strands through the first stitch of your cast-on edge, forming a loop of fringe. Pull the ends of your fringe strands through the loop—you just made a tidy slipknot! Continue to make fringe across entire cast-on edge of your scarf. Repeat for the bound-off edge, trimming the fringe if necessary to make it nice and even.

· ·

Add stripes: (I made all my Magic Scarves in self-striping wool, and they look so pretty—if I do say so myself! And I do.)

How did I get the name for this scarf? I think it's magic the way knits and purls make art. Magic! Or maybe yarn gnomes! Either way, I love you, knitting . . . because you love me back.

Giant Pom-Pom Scarf

INGREDIENTS:

♦ **Yarn:** 1 or 2 skeins worsted-weight yarn (280 yards). I used two skeins of Rio De La Plata worsted hand-dyed wool in "Faded Brick Red" for an extra-long scarf.

♦ **Plus:** 1 skein yarn for the pom-poms (140 yards)

♦ **Needles:** Size 10 straight needles; one large-eye yarn needle for attaching pom-poms to scarf

♦ **Wine Selection:** Cuvée Roucaillat

♦ **Accessories:** Extra-large pom-pom maker (or you can buy premade pom-poms)

THE RECIPE:

Cast on 32 stitches. Work in stockinette stitch for the entire length of the scarf: knit one row, purl the next. Some people will think this is torture, but I like the simplicity of it (it's great for watching TV!).

Note: Stockinette stitch does curl up at the edges, and this is a feature I like; it makes the scarf more of a tube. If you don't like rolled-up sausage stockinette scarves, you could knit this in garter stitch (knit each stitch, each row) or ribbing (knit 2 stitches, purl 2 stitches all the way across).

FINISHING:

When you have reached your desired scarf length, bind off. Make two GIANT pom-poms using a pom-pom maker (available in most knitting and craft stores). Attach one pom-pom to each end of the scarf using the yarn tails left over from tying off the pom-poms. Thread the tails through a large-eye yarn needle, and use the yarn to "sew up" the ends of the scarf, gathering them together into a point (this is easier with a stockinette scarf since it wants to curl up on the edges anyway).

Draw the pom-pom tightly to the end of the scarf and make a sturdy knot. Sew in the ends of the yarn tail near the spot where you joined the pom-pom so it's not visible.

❧ The Faux-Lacy Scarf ☙

Even though this scarf is a super-simple mix of regular old knit stitches and a few yarn-over stitches, it produces a scarf that looks deceptively difficult. When non-knitting people ask me if it was hard to make, I lie right through my teeth and tell them, "Oh, yes, it was so complex! Isn't it pretty!" and I just carry on about it as if I were some great knitter who could make something other than a rectangle.

INGREDIENTS:

- ♦ **Yarn:** 1 skein bulky-weight yarn (I am using Lana Grossa Colore Print yarn in color #005). I've also made this using basic worsted-weight Red Heart and it looked great!

- ♦ **Needles:** Size 13 needles

- ♦ **Beverage Selection:** Newcastle Brown Ale

- ♦ **Special Stitch:** Yarn Over

The yarn over is a simple way to make holes in your fabric; here it looks lacy and airy in the middle of the scarf. To "yarn over" you simply bring the yarn forward and wrap it once around the right needle. It creates a little loop between your real stitches, thus making a hole and creating that airy, lacy look in the middle of this scarf.

THE RECIPE:

Step 1: Cast on 16 stitches.

Step 2: Knit three rows of garter stitch. Garter stitch is when you knit every stitch (no purling). You can knit more or less than three rows depending on how big you'd like the ends of the scarf to be.

Step 3: On the fourth row, and every row for the rest of the scarf (until you get to the other end where you knit the final three rows of plain garter stitch to finish it off all symmetrical-like), you follow this pattern:

> Knit 3 stitches.
> Then, for the middle 10 stitches, do this:
> Yarn over, knit 2 stitches together.
> Yarn over, knit 2 together.
> Yarn over, knit 2 together.
> Yarn over, knit 2 together. (See? So easy!)
> Yarn over, knit 2 together.
> Knit the final 3 stitches of each row.

A Note on Knitting Two Stitches Together: Yes. "Knit 2 together," or K2tog, is a simple decrease, where you knit two stitches together as one. It also serves to keep your stitch count in this lacy scarf from growing out of control with all those yarn overs! Adding a yarn over increases the amount of loops on your knitting needles, so by knitting the two stitches together that come after the yarn over, you create a lovely lacy hole and also don't have a bazillion stitches at the end of the row.

Step 4: Repeat for every row until your scarf is as long as you want, then knit three final rows of garter stitch.

Step 5: Bind off; do a happy dance!

❧ Easy Roll-Brim Hat ☙

Great for covering wrinkles on your forehead.

INGREDIENTS:

♦ **Yarn:** 1 skein Crystal Palace Iceland wool in orange, plus 1 skein Crystal Palace Iceland wool in pink for a stripe

♦ **Needles:** Size 11 circular needles, 16 inches long; size 11 double-pointed needles (SCARY!!!)

♦ **Wine Selection:** Bonterra Organic Cabernet Sauvignon

♦ **Stitch Marker:** I use the heart-shaped ring my parents got me when I was fifteen.

♦ **Goal:** Make a hat from any yarn without a pattern

THE RECIPE:

Start with the Measuring Your Head Formula to get your cast-on going

(Warning: This is the Evil Math!)

Step 1: Measure the circumference of your head. This is best done prior to the wine-drinking.

Step 2: Knit up a small square of fabric using the same yarn you'll use for your hat and the same-sized needles. This little square is called a "gauge swatch." It will tell you how many stitches of knitting are inside one inch of finished fabric.

. . . .

Step 3: Measure the swatch to find stitches per inch.

Step 4: Multiply stitches per inch by head measurement.

My gauge = 3.5 stitches per inch

My head = 21 inches

Ergo, 3.5 x 21 = 73.5

Note: I went with 72 as my amount of cast-on stitches instead of 73 or 74, because it is a number I know how to divide easily (for the decreases), and also because I'm tired of making gigantor hats. Always err on the side of rounding down on the amount of stitches cast on. Hats are supposed to fit a bit snugly.

Step 5: Begin your hat: On a circular needle, cast on the amount of stitches from the Head Formula. I am using 72 stitches.

Step 6: Place a stitch marker on your needle at the end of the last cast-on stitch.

A Note about the Stitch Marker: The first time I knitted "in the round," I couldn't visualize how on earth the stitch marker worked. Was it knitted into the hat? How do you get it out of the stitches? Yes, I am a dumbass. But the stitch marker just gets scooted from one needle to the other as you knit around—you've completed a row when you're back at your marker. Then you scoot it again, from one needle to the other. Use a ring, a piece of string, a rubber band, whatever you want as a stitch marker.

. . . .

A Note about Twisted Stitches: Make sure your stitches are not twisted! That means the knotty-looking part of the stitches are hanging downward and nothing is twisty on your needles.

Step 7: Join the stitches together. Hold the needle with your last cast-on stitch (stitch #72, for me) in the right hand. Hold the needle with the very first cast-on stitch in the left hand. Knit into that first cast-on stitch, and pull the yarn snug so there's no gap. This forms a circle. Let the circle be unbroken!

Note to OCD, Type-A Knitters: My joins always look sloppy. Hopefully I'll get better at this, but look, this is a roll-brim hat. No one will ever see it. MOVE ON.

Step 8: Okay. Here's a tip: Hold your needles toward you. The plastic part (the plastic tubing that makes them "circular") should be sticking out *away* from you. I found out that if you hold the plastic in front, you will be knitting the whole project inside out. Yup. I have no idea how this works either. Magic! Yarn gnomes again! I do not know. And even though I *realize* this is a problem for me—knitting inside out—I still accidentally do it. Whoops! It's no biggie. Just turn your project to the right side once you have a few rows. Who cares, it's just yarn! It loves you!

Step 9: Ask yourself, is this the longest pattern I have ever read or what?

Step 10: Knit every row until you have about 6 to 7 inches of knitting, depending on how much roll you want in the brim. Lay your hat on a table, smooth down the rolling brim, and measure from the cast-on edge up to your most recent stitch. Actually, just try it on. It will make sense.

Stripe Stuff: At some point in the 5- or 6-inch portion, you can switch yarns and make a stripe. Just start knitting with another color at the beginning of a row and knit until you have a big fat stripe. Or skinny stripe. Or whatever floats your stripe boat.

A Note About Adding a Different Color Yarn: When you're ready to add a new color of yarn to any project, cut the yarn off the first color and leave a few inches of yarn tail. (You will weave the ends in later after the hat is completed.)

To add the new yarn color for your stripe, hold the new color of yarn tight and begin knitting a new stitch in the contrast color, leaving a yarn tail of three to five inches (for weaving in later). It's important to hold the yarn tightly as you knit the new stitches in the new color so there aren't any holes or gaps. Some folks find it handy to use the new color of yarn to make a small single knot over the yarn tale of the main color, and go back later, unknot it, and weave in the ends.

Weaving in loose ends is one of my favorite things to do, but I am not normal. Simply use a crochet hook to pull the yarn tail in and under the bar of stitches from the wrong side of your project. Or use a yarn needle to sew the ends in and out underneath your stitches. Snip the ends when you have them sewn in securely.

Step 11: Now you're going to start decreasing. You may want to have your wine selection (or beer) handy, since the double-pointed needles are coming up. I'm just saying, is all.

Step 12: Begin decreasing. Decreasing is pretty simple. You just knit a certain number of stitches, la la la knitting normal, then knit 2 stitches together, and repeat.

To figure out how and when to decrease, you have to do the Evil Math! But it's easy. Just find a smallish number that divides easily into your cast-on stitches number.

Me: I cast on 72 stitches.

72 is divisible by 12.

Now: Math

Here is the scary, genius part of the knitting: You do not even need to know math! Pretend the stitches are shoes. You know all the shoes you cast on (72) are easily divided into groups of 12.

Then, you want to get rid of one pair of shoes by knitting two shoes together. But you're wondering *which two shoes* you knit together, right?

Subtract 2 (shoes) from 12 (shoes): $12 - 2 = 10$

VOILÀ! You decrease by knitting 10 stitches, then knitting 2 stitches together. Continue all the way on the round (knitting 10 and then knitting 2 together), and you're decreasing!!! No stitches get left out in the cold. All the shoes have mates! (I have no idea either, but it works. I swear.)

Step 13: Knit the next round of decreases. So, if you started out by knitting 10, knit 2 together . . . then you knit 9, knit 2 together. And so on.

Step 14: If the previous row was knit 9, knit 2 together, now you decrease by knitting 8, then knit 2 together.

Step 15: This pattern, the SIMPLE roll-brim hat? We're on Step 15 already. Ha ha.

Step 16: Here they come: The DPNs of D—double-pointed needles of death.

Deep breath. Sigh with the weight of the world. Drink wine. Begin switching to three double-pointed needles.

Me? I'm a big, fat weenie and not a super-advanced knitter (yet!), so here's how I first made the transition from a circular needle to double-pointed needles—I slipped the stitches off my circs and onto my double-points without knitting them, evenly distributing stitches over the three double-pointed needles.

It's just a transition step. That way I didn't have to combine decreasing and counting with knitting onto the scary double-pointed needles and cussing and sipping wine and trying to get a cat off my lap all at the same time. It may take a few minutes more in the long run, but at this point we're on Step 16, and what's a few more minutes? Really, now?

OR, Alternately: You can knit the stitches off your circulars with your double-points. This is what I do now, but it took me six hats and much wine to get comfortable with it.

Step 17: Now everything is on the double-pointed needles. Your pack of needles should either have four or five needles. You're only using three to hold the hat stitches. So, with the leftover double-pointed needle, begin knitting off the double-points. Basically you knit as if with straight needles, taking the stitches off a full double-point and onto an empty double-pointed needle.

Step 18: Keep on decreasing until you cannot stand it anymore. I usually decrease down until I only have about 10 to 12 stitches on my needles.

Step 19: Cut your yarn, leaving about 8 inches of yarn tail for pulling the whole thing together. Thread the tail through a yarn needle and pull it tightly through all the remaining stitches, gathering them tight and closing the hole at the top of the hat. Make a knot. Weave in all ends.

Step 20: Finally! "Easy" hat. Embellish with a pom-pom, if desired. Drink wine and feel happy as pie. Imagine you are a superior knitter, with superior hat-making skills. Avoid all news channels that tell you about global warming, negating the need for a wool hat.

Enjoy!

⚐ Cat Tunnel ⚐

My cats love to lay around on my knitting, decorating each project with their own unique cat hair contributions. I thought it was high time I make them their own knitted masterpiece. This project is just miles and miles of stockinette in the round and there is no shaping and no fancy stitches, so it's perfect for a wine-infused evening with a good movie and yes, even a cat on your lap. The very best part of this knitted cat toy is that it involves a trip to the hardware store. I myself have had very good luck with helpful employees of the local hardware store, indeed!

NOTE BEFORE YOU BEGIN:

This project is really just a big, knitted cozy for a cardboard tube. The knitted piece you'll create covers the outside of a large cardboard tube and then folds inside it as well, covering it completely with knitted fabric. Since each cardboard tube can vary tremendously in exact circumference, it's very important to knit a swatch of fabric before you begin and to measure it carefully. To double-check on size and mathyness, I knitted about four inches of my cat tunnel cover and slipped it on over the tube just to be sure it wasn't way too big.

INGREDIENTS:

♦ **Yarn:** 3–4 skeins Lion Brand Wool-Ease Thick 'n Quick (varies depending on the length of your cat tunnel)

. . . .

Hardware:

♦ One large, sturdy cardboard tube. I used a Quik-Tube™ concrete-pouring tube from the contractor supplies aisle of my local hardware store. This pattern was created using the 12" diameter tube. The label states clearly that each tube varies + or − 5" in circumference.

♦ One sturdy cardboard cutter or hacksaw for trimming the length of your tube.

♦ **Needles:** Size 13, 29-inch circular needle, large-eye yarn needle for finishing (or crochet hook)

♦ **Accessories:** Large-size pom-pom maker (optional)

♦ **Beverage Selection:** Mint Juleps, or warm mint tea if it's cold outside.

THE RECIPE:

Step 1: With a soft tape measure, carefully measure around the outside of your cardboard tube. You are measuring around the *circumference* of the tube, not measuring it length-wise. The length of your finished project depends on how much stomach you have for yards and yards of stockinette knitting!

My tube measured 38.5" around, and in this project it's best to round down on your measurement. So we'll call it 38" in width.

Step 2: Knit a small gauge swatch to determine how many stitches per inch you're knitting. For my swatch, I cast on about 25 stitches

. . . .

and knit in stockinette stitch for about ten rows, then I bound off the swatch. Lay the small piece of knitted fabric out carefully on a flat surface (pin the edges if it starts to roll up on you) and then using a small ruler, measure somewhere in the middle of the fabric to see how many stitches you get per inch of knitted fabric. I got two stitches per inch on my swatch.

Step 3: Super-simple cast-on math time! Multiply your stitches-per-inch (in my case it was 2 stitches) by the amount of inches you'll be covering on that cardboard tube (for me we're using 38") and that final number is a roundabout cast on number. Mine is 2 x 38 = 76, but because I want the knitted sleeve to fit a little snugly on my tunnel, I'm going to cast on 74 stitches instead of 76.

Step 4: Cast on your desired amount of stitches and join them in the round. Begin knitting in the round for what may seem like an eternity.

Step 5: This project can be any length you want. I am knitting a two-foot-long cat tunnel for my felines. Because the knitted fabric covers not just the outside but also the inside of the tube, you will be knitting twice the length of the cat tunnel. I was not kidding with the miles of stockinette.

Step 6: When you can no longer move your fingers from all the knitting OR when you've gotten a tube of knitted fabric twice the length of your desired tunnel length, bind off. You can either weave in the ends here or use them to sew the tunnel together.

Step 7: Cut the cardboard tube to the exact right length. To do this, I folded my knitted tube in half lengthwise (I knitted four feet of fabric, so I folded it in half to about two feet of fabric) and slide it on over the cardboard tube. Mark on the cardboard tube where the knitted tunnel covers, then add about ? an inch extra – we want the knitted fabric to stretch a bit down the length of the cardboard and fit very snugly. Remove the knitted fabric and set aside.

Step 8: CAREFULLY cut the cardboard tube to desired length. I used a hacksaw but you could probably use a sturdy box cutter as well.

Step 9: Put the knitted tube over the cardboard tube. Drop the excess fabric INSIDE the tube, so the cardboard is now fully encased in stockinette knitting. Bet the contractor's section of the hardware store didn't have THIS in mind when they sold me that tube!

Step 10: Sew the edges of the knitted tube together. You can use any stitch you're comfortable with, since you can maneuver the tube where the seam is inside (and only the cats will see it there). I used a plain whipstitch with leftover yarn and a large-eye yarn needle to sew mine together.

Step 11: (Optional) Make six or eight huge pom-poms and sew them to the bottom sides of the tube like caterpillar legs. This can help stabilize the tube from rolling, although my cats tend to attack the pompoms. You can also use spray catnip to lace the inside of the tunnel with cat-loving fun smells.

Step 12: Get a hand massage. Four hundred miles of knitting for a damn cat toy . . . you deserve it!

Wide-Rib Brim Hat

Great for bad hair days. During the "crazy time," I think I wore my hat for an entire week without washing—the hat . . . or myself.

INGREDIENTS:

♦ **Yarn:** 1 skein Lion Brand Wool Ease Thick 'n Quick in black

♦ **Note:** I managed to get by on 1 skein . . . just barely. I think I had about four feet of yarn left over. So buy 2 skeins if you can, just for peace of mind.

♦ **Needles:** Size 10 circular needles, 16-inch length; size 11 circular needles, 16-inch length; size 11 double-pointed needles of death (not that scary)

♦ **Wine Selection:** A fizzy Cava will help you forget your hair.

♦ **Accessories:** Stitch marker; feline assistant (optional)

THE RECIPE:

Step 1: Using the smaller (size 10) circular needle, cast on 64 stitches. Using a smaller needle on the ribbed area keeps the ribbing from poufing out and makes the final hat look more finished. Also remember that in circular knitting, you cast on exactly the same way as in straight knitting. It's easy! You can do it. I use the long-tail cast-on method, but use any cast-on you are comfortable with. It's a hat, not world peace.

Step 2: Place a stitch marker on the right needle. Look at your stitches: all the knotty parts should be smoothly pointing in the same direction and nothing should be twisting around the loopy part of your circular needle.

Step 3: Join the stitches into a circular tube of knitting happiness by knitting into the stitch on the left needle. This starts your first row of ribbing!

Step 4: Make the big ribbed hat brim: knit 4 stitches, then purl 4 stitches all the way across the round (rows are called "rounds" in circular knitting. They're still rows. But I'm going with the lingo).

And that's it!

It's easy. Knit 4, purl 4 all the way around and around until you have knitted approximately 4.5 inches of ribbing. (That's obviously more ribbing than gets turned up for a brim on this hat, but I like to have more ribbing than I need; this way, if I adjust the brim while I'm wearing it, I don't get a piece of stockinette sticking out.)

TO MEASURE THE RIBBING: Lay the hat on a flat surface, smoothing it with your hand and checking it on a ruler. This portion took me approximately one and a half hours to knit, but I was knitting on the bus, and I am a slow knitter. Your mileage may vary.

Step 5: Switch to your larger circular needle (size 11) for the stockinette body.

Switching needles isn't as hard as it sounds. You have completed your last ribbing row. This part of the hat—where the ribbing meets the road—will not be visible when you wear the hat, because the brim turns up about 3 inches into the ribbing, so don't worry if your knitting gets a little weird on this one row.

So—first, knit one stitch on this row with your size 10 needle just like normal to "seal" the stitch marker in (I hate having a dangling stitch marker hanging off the end of that small size 10 needle as I'm swapping to size 11s—trust me, this will make sense when you do it). Next, using your bigger size 11 needle, begin knitting the remaining stitches off the left-hand size 10 (smaller) needle.

Step 6: With all stitches on the bigger needles, knit every single stitch on every row until you have 3 inches of stockinette. Isn't knitting in the round awesome?! Perfect stockinette from the knit stitch! I love it!

Step 7: Decrease stitches. Once you have 3 inches of stockinette, begin decreasing: Knit 14 stitches. Then knit 2 together. Continue this (knit 14, knit 2 together) all the way across the round. You will end with 60 stitches.

Tip: Definitely put a stitch marker right after your knit-2-together decrease. This helps because we're going to decrease on every single row for the next thirteen rows, and if you place a marker after each decrease, you'll always know when you're supposed to be knitting 2 stitches together—knit the 2 stitches before each marker together.

Next row: Knit 13, knit 2 together all across the round. You will have 56 stitches on your needles when you finish the round.

Step 8: Right about here you will want to switch to double-pointed needles. It's not that hard—if a goofball like me can figure it out, so can you! You use the double-pointed needles in place of a circular one because that loopy plastic part of a circular needle will be too long once you have fewer stitches. You can also do crazy Magic Loop stuff with two circular needles, but this is the way I do it. Makes me feel like an extreme knitter with all those sticks!

Knit about one-third of the stitches onto the first double-pointed needle (keep up with your decreases). I never worry if I have the stitches in exact, even numbers on each needle, because I am a lazy and freewheelin' knitter. I am the knitter your mama warned you about. Luckily, this weird "guestimate" trick works wonders, preventing any weird gaps when using double-pointed needles, because I always have to scoot stitches from one needle to the next to get my "knit 2 together" to work out.

Just knit all your stitches onto three or four double-pointed needles. Then, with the free double-pointed needle, begin knitting as if you were straight knitting. Cool, huh? Every time you free up a needle, use that as your new right-hand needle. You can do this.

Continue with the hat as follows, repeating all the way across each round: Knit 12, knit 2 together (all the way to the end of the round). You end with 52 stitches.

Knit 11, knit 2 together. End with 48 stitches.

Knit 10, knit 2 together. End with 44 stitches.

Knit 9, knit 2 together. End with 40 stitches.

Knit 8, knit 2 together. End with 36 stitches.

Knit 7, knit 2 together. End with 32 stitches.

Knit 6, knit 2 together. End with 28 stitches.

Knit 5, knit 2 together. End with 24 stitches.

Knit 4, knit 2 together. End with 20 stitches.

Knit 3, knit 2 together. End with 16 stitches.

Knit 2, knit 2 together. End with 12 stitches.

Step 9: Finish up! Cut the yarn tail, leaving about 10 inches of yarn. Thread the yarn through a large-eye needle and pull it tightly through all the remaining stitches on your needles to close the gap.

I sometimes run the needle through the stitches twice because I am a paranoid, neurotic knitter. Draw the top closed, bring the yarn to the wrong side of the hat, turn your hat inside out, and weave in your ends. I sometimes tie a knot, too, just because (see "paranoid, neurotic").

Step 10: Wear hat; pose everywhere for paparazzi.

Easy Felted Bracelet Bag

This little number is perfect for a night out on the town or your first "real" date in over a year. Just remember to put in enough money for a cab in case the guy turns out to be not worth your time.

THE INSPIRATION:

I wanted a little, teensy handbag to take out at night—just enough room for my ID, lipstick, small compact, money, and keys. Enter the bracelet bag, a perfect solution! I created this whole bag on the fly while sitting on my sofa and watching Jaws on TV. By the time Richard Dreyfuss and Roy Scheider were paddling back to Amity Island, I was done with all the knitting—including sewing the sides up—and was ready to felt it.

INGREDIENTS:

- **Yarn:** ½ skein any chunky 100% wool yarn that can be felted (no superwash wool!) and ½ skein any eyelash, ribbon, or glittery yarn to jazz up the bag (optional)

- **Needles:** Size 13 needles, large-eye yarn needle, and regular sewing needle (and thread)

- **Accessories:** Two bangle bracelets for the handle (I wouldn't use elastic bracelets because they might stretch out or break); cheesy afternoon movie

- **Beverage Selection:** Fresca

♦ **Pep Talk:** The hard part of this recipe—which isn't very hard *at all*, mind you—comes in the first few rows. You start knitting at one end of the bag, making the tabs that will eventually fold over your bracelets. Then you increase stitches to make a triangle that leads to a plain rectangle, knit the rectangle, and start decreasing on the other end for the other tab. (Decreasing is so easy—you just knit 2 stitches together.)

THE RECIPE:

Step 1: If you are using a sparkle or eyelash yarn for jazzing-up purposes, hold the wool and the fancy yarn together and knit with them like they are one yarn. One yarn, one world.

Cast on 4 stitches.

Row 1: Knit 4.

Row 2: Purl 4.

Row 3: Knit 4.

Row 4: Purl 4.

Step 2: Start increasing stitches on each row to get to the desired width of the bag.

For this pattern, I increased by doing a "make 1" increase, which is actually pretty simple. Every time you see "make 1" in the pattern, just knit the next stitch, but don't pull it off the left needle to finish it. Instead, go back to the same stitch on the left needle, and now knit into it *through the back loop*. That just means you stick your knitting needle into the back leg of the stitch instead of the front leg, knit it, and pull it off the needle. You now have 2 stitches that came from 1! This increase can make a little hole. But when using bulky yarn and felting it anyway, there will be no holes after it's all shrunken and felty.

Row 5: Knit 1, make 1 by knitting in the front and back of next stitch, make 1 again on the next stitch, knit 1. You now have 6 stitches.

Row 6: Purl 6.

Row 7: Knit 2, make 1, make 1, knit 2. You now have 8 stitches.

Row 8: Purl 8.

Row 9: Knit 2, make 1, knit 2, make 1, knit 2 (10 stitches).

Row 10: Purl 10.

Row 11: Knit 1, make 1, knit 2, make 1, make 1 again, knit 2, make 1, knit 1 (14 stitches).

Row 12: Purl 14.

Row 13: Knit 2, make 1, knit 2, make 1, knit 2, make 1, knit 2, make 1, knit 2. You now have 18 stitches—and you are done increasing!!!

Row 14: Purl 18.

Now you have made it through the only hard part of this bag!

Step 3: For the next 12 to 14 inches of knitting (depending on how deep/long you want your handbag to be), simply knit in plain stockinette stitch. That's where you knit one row, and purl the next row. I knitted 12 inches. Your bag will begin to curl up, looking like a weird banana.

Make sure you end this portion by finishing up a PURL row.

Step 4: Starting with a KNIT row, begin decreasing. You only need to knit fourteen more rows to finish this whole bag, so I'll go back to basic numbering starting with the first decrease row. You should have 18 stitches on your needles.

Row 1: Knit 2, knit 2 together, all the way across the row. Then knit the final 2 stitches. You should have 14 stitches now.

Row 2: Purl 14.

Row 3: Knit 1, knit 2 together, knit 2, knit 2 together, knit 2 together again, knit 2, knit 2 together, knit the final stitch. Now there are 10 stitches.

Row 4: Purl 10.

Row 5: Knit 2, knit 2 together across the row, then knit the final 2 stitches (8 stitches remain).

Row 6: Purl 8.

Row 7: Knit 2, knit 2 together, knit another 2 together, knit 2 (6 stitches left).

Row 8: Purl 6.

Row 9: Knit 1, knit 2 together, knit 2 together again, knit final stitch (4 stitches—woohoo!).

Step 5: Make tab.

Row 10: Purl 4.

Row 11: Knit 4.

Row 12: Purl 4.

Row 13: Knit 4.

Step 6: Bind off.

Step 7: Weave in ends. You don't have to be neat here—the ends will "felt in."

Step 8: Fold the bag in half with the tabs together at the top. It should be inside out, with the bumpy reverse-stockinette stitch on the outside. Seam up the sides—pin the bag together at the sides. Cut a piece of the wool yarn, about 15 inches long. Thread this through your large-eye yarn needle and whipstitch the sides of the bag together. You can be messy; the whole thing gets felted anyway.

Step 9: You're all done constructing the bag! Turn the bag right side out again and get ready to felt it.

FELTING THE BAG:

Step 1: Place the bag inside a pillowcase and use a rubber band or hair elastic to close up the pillowcase real tight. You don't want fuzz and fluff from your bag clogging up the washer.

Step 2: Throw the sealed pillowcase in with a load of towels or jeans. I washed this bag on permanent press—hot wash, cold rinse. I didn't care if it shrank down a lot. I added some detergent and let the entire wash cycle run, including the spin cycle. I'm a reckless felter, what can I say? Your mileage may vary—so if you don't want this bag to shrink too much, start out on a cold wash cycle and check the progress about halfway through the wash.

Step 3: That's it! Take the bag out of the washer, shape it with your hands, and let it dry on a dish towel in the kitchen.

FINALLY, ADD THE BRACELET HANDLES:

When your bag is fully dry, fold the tabs down over the bracelets and sew each tab in place using regular sewing thread and a needle. Go out, drink up, enjoy!

❧ Flower Pom-Pom ❦

Making the flower pom-pom is really easy. It's made just like an old-school regular pom-pom, but you don't cut the ends.

I first learned how to make pom-poms when I was in the fifth grade and was obsessed with roller skating. The roller-skating rink in our town sold pink and green pom-poms with bells for $12 a pair. I coveted a set of bell pom-poms, because you put them on the toe laces of your skates. We couldn't afford the astronomical price, of course (*twelve whole dollars!*) and neither could a lot of my friends, so we made our own.

We didn't have a pom-pom maker like you can buy in the stores now (in fact, until I started knitting, I didn't know there was such a thing!), and while I definitely use my store-bought pom-pom maker now for traditional toppers, this flower pom-pom only needs yarn and a "guide" made from a sturdy postcard or a piece of cardboard approximately 6 inches long and 3.5 inches tall.

This works best with bulkier yarns.

INGREDIENTS:

♦ **Yarn:** Bulky yarn in any color plus scrap yarn to tie the middle

♦ **Accessories:** Pom-pom "guide" and scissors

♦ **Beverage Selection:** Limeade like in the roller rink days (You can also add vodka to the limeade)

THE RECIPE:

Step 1: Wrap a whole bunch of yarn around the guide in a mostly even layer (not wrapped in a bulge all in one place).

Step 2: Once you have a good amount of yarn wrapped, carefully slide the yarn off the guide. Pinch it in the middle.

Step 3: Use a small piece of yarn to tie the whole bunch in the center.

Step 4: Fluff into a rounded shape! Voilà! Use to embellish any object that stands still long enough, such as hats, wineglasses, and felines.

Stashbuster Flower

By Allison Keech Sanka, SuperCrafty.com

This is a fast and easy knitted flower pin pattern, suitable for a beginning knitter. You can make a pin or use them to decorate purses, hats, and scarves. One skein of yarn will yield several flowers. This pattern is great for using up partial skeins, stash, or that stray ball of novelty yarn you found under the couch or in the cat bed. The finished size is approximately 3.5 to 4 inches in diameter.

INGREDIENTS:

+ **Flower Base:** 1 skein of worsted or heavy worsted-weight yarn. Exact gauge is not important, but should be roughly 4–5 stitches per inch. Use size 7 or 8 single point needles, crochet hook for finishing, tapestry/yarn needle, craft pin back (if making into a brooch) to complete this project.

+ **Beaded Decoration:** Beading needle (very thin), clear nylon thread, five freshwater pearl or other beads.

THE RECIPE:

+ Cast on 5 stitches, knit 1 row.

+ **Next 4 rows:** Knit 1, increase 1 stitch, knit to end of row.

+ There should be 9 stitches. Knit 4 rows.

+ **Next 6 rows:** Knit 1, k2tog decrease, knit to end of row.

- Three stitches remain. Knit 1 row and then bind off. On two petals, leave 12-inch tail.

- Repeat to make five identical pieces.

FINISHING:

Arrange the five petals in circular formation so that the right edge of each petal lies exposed, overlaying the petal on the right. Pulling the tails downward to the back of the flower, tie the tails together in a knot. You may have to rearrange the petals again so the right edges are exposed.

Thread the tapestry needle with about 12 inches of waste yarn or the tail of one petal. Sew the right edge of each petal down to the petal it overlaps, following the knit stitch pattern so that the stitches are not visible.

Thread the bead needle with a double strand of clear nylon thread, and starting from back to front, sew through the center of the flower a few times to secure the thread. String on each of five beads, sewing each down onto the center of the flower.

If desired, sew on pin back with one tail of yarn.

Weave in the ends.

ABOUT ALLISON KEECH SANKA:

Allison Keech Sanka has always been crafty: sewing, embroidery, even woodworking among her creative passions. In 2002, she started knitting to relieve stress from her marketing job at a large entertainment corporation, and a yarn addiction quickly ensued. Allison decided to combine the dream of owning her own business with her love of crafts. In 2004, she left her day job and opened SuperCrafty.com, an online store offering fun, offbeat, and fashion-forward craft supplies and yarns. Allison lives and knits in Los Angeles with her husband Jefferson and son Evan.

Hand-Knit Handbag

By Drew Emborsky, thecrochetdude.com

Drew is my best guy friend. Every girl needs a best guy friend to consult on dating matters, because no matter how much we try to convince ourselves that thirty hours of analysis with our closest girlfriends will yield results on WHY THAT GUY I DATED HAS NOT CALLED ME BACK ALREADY, your best guy friend will tell you the truth, and it will only take a minute and a half. In addition to informing me of the harsh realities of GuyLand, Drew is also a wicked knitter and crocheter extraordinaire, and he makes handbags that are so darn cute you can't stand it.

INGREDIENTS:

- **Yarn:** 5 oz bulky yarn
- **Needles:** Size 11 needles
- **Accessories:** (2) 5.5-inch "flower power"–shaped handles or purse handles of your choosing

THE RECIPE:

Cast on 30 stitches.

Rows 1–3: K

Row 4: WS *P2tog without letting the sts drop, P again into first st letting both sts drop off needle.* Repeat from * to * across.

Row 5: K

Row 6: P1. Repeat row 4 from * to *; end with P1.

Row 7: K

Repeat rows 4–7 one more time.

Begin decreasing:

Row 1: P

Row 2: *k2tog, K2* across ending with k2tog.

Rows 3–4: Repeat rows 1–2.

Row 5: P

Rows 6–9: K

Bind off.

ASSEMBLY:

With wrong sides facing, whipstitch sides and bottom of purse. Turn right side out. Whipstitch handles to top of purse.

ABOUT DREW EMBORSKY:

Drew Emborsky's quirky title as "The Crochet Dude" and his kitschy tongue-in-cheek designs have made him a household name in the fiber design world. His unique role as a male knitter and crochetier has opened doors for other men who were stuck in the closet with their yarn, knitting needles, and crochet hooks. Drew studied fine art at Kendall College of Art & Design in Grand Rapids, Michigan. He coauthored *Men Who Knit and the Dogs Who Love Them* and his latest book of men's clothing designs will be published in 2008. Drew offers patterns and a peek at his day-to-day life at www.blog.thecrochetdude.com. He lives in Houston, Texas with his two cats, Chandler and Cleocatra.

☙ Devil Baby Blanket ☙

By Sara Neff

It seems that as soon as you get the divorce paperwork rolling, every single friend and cousin you know is suddenly pregnant, settling down, and nesting. My friend Sara Neff created this baby blanket pattern, and it is the ideal baby shower gift for those first-time expectant mothers who clearly have no idea what they are getting into, or for more experienced mothers who know exactly what they are getting into.

Sara says she abhors weaving in ends, so she minimized that throughout this pattern by tucking many of them conveniently in between the sides of the horns and the sides of the tail. Clever girl!

INGREDIENTS:

♦ **Yarn:** MC: 2 skeins Caron Simply Soft #9730 Autumn Red (100% acrylic; 330 yards per 6 oz skein); CC: 1 skein Patons Brilliant #4942 Radiant Red (69% acrylic, 31% polyester, 166 yards per 50g)

♦ **Needles:** Size 8 3-inch circular needle; 2 size #8/5mm double-pointed needles

♦ **Gauge:** 16 sts and 23 rows = 4 inches in stockinette (row gauge is not so important in this pattern, so if you don't get 23 sts, don't sweat it)

♦ **Notions:** Safety pins, tapestry needle, and crochet hook size F

THE RECIPE:

BLANKET:

CO 3 stitches.

Row 1: knit.

Row 2: K1, M1, K to 2 sts from end, M1, K1.

Repeat rows 1 and 2 until you have 25 sts on your needle.

Increase Rows

Row 3: K12, PM, P1, PM, K12.

Row 4: K12, sl marker, M1, K to next marker, M1, sl marker, K12.

Row 5: K12, sl marker, P to next marker, sl marker, K12.

Repeat rows 4 and 5 until you have 153 sts, or your piece measures 27 inches on a side (not along the diagonal row of your stitches, but along the outer edge).

Decrease Rows

Row 6: K12, sl marker, ssk, K to next marker, k2tog, sl marker, K12.

Row 7: K12, sl marker, P to next marker, sl marker, K12.

Repeat rows 4 and 5 until you have 25 sts left.

FINAL BLANKET ROWS:

Row 8: K1, ssk, K to 3 before end, k2tog, K1, removing markers on the first row.

Row 9: K.

Repeat rows 8 and 9 until you have 3 stitches left.

BO.

HOOD:

Work as for blanket until hood measures 12 inches along the diagonal (not along the side like you measured earlier).

Next RS row (to create a turning row): K12, sl marker, P to next marker, sl marker, K12.

Work 2 more rows in patt.

BO.

Using a tapestry needle and CC, sew the BO stitches in the stockinette section to the underside of the hood two rows underneath, so that the edge that would otherwise curl up is sewn underneath.

ASSEMBLY:

Using safety pins, pin the hood to the corner of the blanket on which you CO. Using CC, sc around the entire edge of the blanket, starting at the BO corner. When you reach the next blanket corner, sc 3 times in the stitch on the outside that corresponds to the stockinette corner, as this will help the corner have a more "cornery" shape. When you work your way up to the hood, you will sc the hood and the blanket together and then head back down to the BO corner, remembering to put 3 sc stitches in the third corner on your way down. This makes more sense in the diagram.

sc along the edge of the hood.

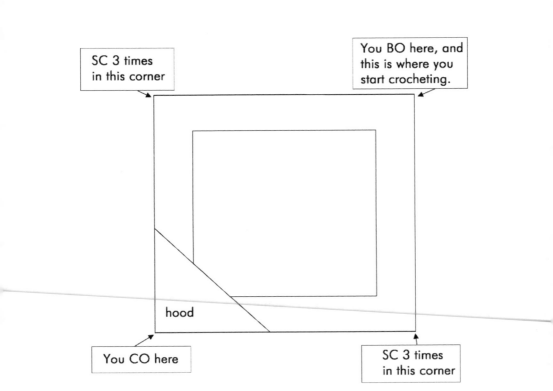

SC 3 times
in this corner

You BO here, and
this is where you
start crocheting.

hood

You CO here

SC 3 times
in this corner

DEVIL HORNS (MAKE 4)

With either set of needles (it doesn't really matter), and with MC
and CC held together, CO 5 sts. Leave a long enough tail for this
CO to sew the devil horn to the baby blanket (less ends to weave in
that way).

Work 4 rows garter stitch.

*K3, k2tog

K 1 row *

Rep from * to * once more, 3 sts remaining

**k2tog, kfb

K 1 row**.

Rep from ** to ** once more.

Cut yarn, draw through 3 rem sts.

TO ATTACH DEVIL HORNS TO BLANKET:

Use long CO tail to sew one of the horns to the side of the hood of
the blanket, and then sew the other on the other side of the horn you
just sewed. Don't even bother weaving in any of the ends; just tuck
them in between the two horns to give them a bit of bulk.

Using CC, sc around horn to attach the two sides of the horn to each
other. Repeat for other side.

DEVIL TAIL:

With MC and CC held together, P 4 stitches on BO corner. Using
dpn, K 25 inches of I-cord. BO, leaving enough yarn to attach the
tail to the devil point.

· ·

DEVIL POINT (MAKE 2):

With either set of needles (it doesn't really matter): CO 1 st.

K 1 row.

Next row: kfb, 2 sts.

K 1 row.

Next row: kfb, 4 sts.

K 2 rows.

Next row: *kfb, K to last st kfb.

K 1 row * rep from * to * once more.

Next row: *kfb, K to last st kfb.

K 2 rows* rep from * to * 3 times more, 16 sts.

Next row: K6, k2tog, turn, placing remaining sts on holder.

** K 1 row.

Next row: k2tog, K3, k2tog, turn.

K 1 row.

Next row: k2tog, K1, k2tog, turn.

BO.**

Transfer holder sts to needle. Join yarn and k2tog, K6.

Rep from ** to **.

Using CC, sc the two sides of the devil tail to each other. Again, do not bother weaving in any ends. Just tuck them in between the sides.

Use the yarn left over from binding off the tail to sew the tail to the devil point. Use the tapestry needle to bring up any leftover yarn into the devil point so you don't have to weave that in either.

· ·

Using the tapestry needle and the CC, sew the devil tail to the baby blanket in a squiggly line, as shown in the (expertly drawn) diagram below.

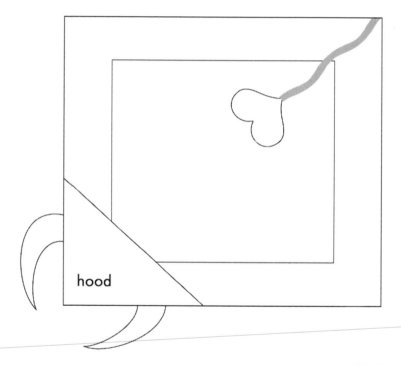

hood

Weave in any extra ends, and voilà! You have created the perfect baby gift for Judgment Day!

ABOUT SARA NEFF

Sara's mother taught her how to knit (poorly) when she was in fifth grade, which only resulted in a few well-intentioned, if strangely executed scarves. Fortunately, about five years ago the lovely knitters of Santa Monica and West Hollywood Stitch 'n Bitch bestowed their yarny prowess upon her, and she has been knitting fiendishly ever since. When she is not knitting, she can be found either practicing her saxophone, playing Frisbee, or doing improv while she "works real hard on her graduate school applications."

❧ Sexy Shawl ❧

By Staci Perry, www.verypink.com

This dressy, lacy shawl pattern was created by my friend Staci Perry, a master knitter who can create works of art with yarn. This is a more advanced pattern than my usual garter knit scarf or stockinette in the round hat, but the result is a classic, airy lace shawl perfect for keeping your shoulders warm on a first date.

INGREDIENTS:

+ **Yarn:** 11 50g balls of Louisa Harding Grace (50% Merino wool, 50% silk, 110 yds/100 meters per ball)

+ **Needles:** Size US 3/3.25 mm (or size to obtain gauge)

+ **Accessories:** Stitch markers, row counter, tapestry needle for weaving in ends, crochet hook (size E, F, or G) to attach fringe

+ **Gauge:** 5.5 stitches and 7.5 rows to the inch, unblocked

+ **Finished Measurements:** Length: 68 inches; width: 19 inches

STITCH GUIDE:

+ The seed stitch sections alternate K, P, K, P, K, P, K, P, K across on both RS and WS rows. There are 9 stitches in this section that always begin and end with a K.

+ **SK2P:** slip one stitch, knit next two stitches together, pass slipped stitch over the k2tog, 2 stitches decreased.

+ **PM:** place marker

THE RECIPE:

CO 109 stitches.

Setup row: Starting with a K, work seed stitch for 9 stitches, PM, *P2, PM, K4, YO, SK2P, YO, K4, PM* repeat between asterisks two times more, P2, PM, work seed stitch for 9 stitches, PM, repeat between asterisks three times, P2, PM, work seed stitch for 9 stitches.

Row 2 and all WS rows: Work seed stitch for 9 stitches, *K2, P11* repeat between asterisks two times more, K2, work seed stitch for 9 stitches, repeat between asterisks three times, K2, work seed stitch for 9 stitches.

Row 3: Work seed stitch for 9 stitches, *P2, K3, YO, K1, SK2P, K1, YO, K3*, repeat between asterisks two times more, P2, PM, work seed stitch for 9 stitches, PM, repeat between asterisks three times, work seed stitch for 9 stitches.

Row 5: Work seed stitch for 9 stitches, *P2, K2, YO, K2, SK2P, K2, YO, K2*, repeat between asterisks two times more, P2, PM, work seed stitch for 9 stitches, PM, repeat between asterisks three times, work seed stitch for 9 stitches.

Row 7: Work seed stitch for 9 stitches, *P2, K1, YO, K3, SK2P, K3, YO, K1*, repeat between asterisks two times more, P2, PM, work seed stitch for 9 stitches, PM, repeat between asterisks three times, work seed stitch for 9 stitches.

Row 9: Work seed stitch for 9 stitches, *P2, YO, K4, SK2P, K4, YO*, repeat between asterisks two times more, P2, PM, work seed stitch for 9 stitches, PM, repeat between asterisks three times, work seed stitch for 9 stitches.

Row 11: Repeat row 7.

Row 13: Repeat row 5.

Row 15: Repeat row 3.

Continue in this pattern, replacing the setup row with the following:

Row 1: Work seed stitch for 9 stitches, *K4, YO, SK2P, YO, K4*, repeat between asterisks two times more, P2, PM, work seed stitch for 9 stitches, PM, repeat between asterisks three times, work seed stitch for 9 stitches.

Repeat these 16 rows 29 times, and then work row 1 once more.

BO row (WS): To create the same points as the CO row, there are increases in the BO row. BO first 9 stitches in seed stitch, BO next two in K, BO 4 in P, now you are at the first YO of the last row. In the YO stitch, P in the back of the stitch without pulling it off the left needle, BO that stitch. P in the front of the same stitch, BO that stitch (1 stitch increased, 2 stitches bound off from same stitch). In the next stitch (center of lace pattern), P into the back of the stitch without pulling it off the left needle, BO that stitch. P again into the back of the center stitch without pulling it off the left needle, BO that stitch. P into the front of the same stitch, BO that stitch (2 stitches increased, 3 stitches bound off from same stitch). The next stitch is the second YO of the last row—repeat same P in back, BO, P in front, BO as you did with the first one. Continue in this manner across all stitches.

LACE PATTERN CHART (INCLUDES BORDERING P STITCHES)

#	#	X	X	X	X	X	X	X	X	X	X	X	#	#	16
#	#	X	X	X	O	X	@	X	O	X	X	X	#	#	15
#	#	X	X	X	X	X	X	X	X	X	X	X	#	#	14
#	#	X	X	O	X	X	@	X	X	O	X	X	#	#	13
#	#	X	X	X	X	X	X	X	X	X	X	X	#	#	12
#	#	X	O	X	X	X	@	X	X	X	O	X	#	#	11
#	#	X	X	X	X	X	X	X	X	X	X	X	#	#	10
#	#	O	X	X	X	O	@	O	X	X	X	O	#	#	9
#	#	X	X	X	X	X	X	X	X	X	X	X	#	#	8
#	#	X	O	X	X	X	@	X	X	X	O	X	#	#	7
#	#	X	X	X	X	X	X	X	X	X	X	X	#	#	6
#	#	X	X	O	X	X	@	X	X	X	X	X	#	#	5
#	#	X	X	X	X	X	X	X	X	X	X	X	#	#	4
#	#	X	X	X	O	X	@	X	O	O	X	X	#	#	3
#	#	X	X	X	X	X	X	X	X	X	X	X	#	#	2
#	#	X	X	X	X	O	@	O	X	X	X	X	#	#	1

[Table key] X = K on RS, P on WS; O = YO; # = P on RS, K on WS; @ = SK2P

FINISHING:

Weaving Ends: Use tapestry needle to weave in ends. If you're using the recommended yarn (or any 100% non-superwash animal fiber), you can "spit splice" the new balls of yarn in to keep the number of ends down to two—just the CO and BO tails! Yay!

Fringe: Cut 32 lengths of yarn, 7 inches each. Using crochet hook and two pieces of yarn per fringe, attach fringe at each of the six lace points and both ends (eight fringe attachments at CO and BO rows).

Blocking: Wet block and lay flat to dry. Use pins to really stretch out the points in the lace at both ends. The shawl will grow substantially with blocking, so be sure to check the measurements.

ABOUT STACI PERRY

Staci Perry lives in Houston, Texas, with her four Basenji dogs. She's been knitting, crocheting, and designing since she was seven years old. Staci doesn't remember learning to knit, but believes she was taught because she was annoying her grandmother. When she's not knitting, she can be found walking the dogs or volunteering time for Basenji Rescue. You can read more about Staci and the spoiled dogs (who eat yarn at any given chance), at www.verypink.com.

 Cabled Bucket Bag

By Annie Modesitt

Size(s): One size

Finished Measurement: 19-inch diameter x 10 inches high

INGREDIENTS:

- **Yarn A:** 1 ball of Malabrigo Chunky (1 single strand) (104yds/71m, 3.5oz/100gr per skein; source for Malabrigo yarn: www.malabrigoyarn.com)

- **Color:** Cosecha 229

- **Yarn B:** 1 ball of Malabrigo Merino Worsted (2 strands held together)

- (216yds/197m, 3.5oz/100gr)

- **Color:** Amber Gold 153

Gauge is not vital on this project.

Note: Yarn B is to be DOUBLED when used in this bag. This means you will knit holding two strands of yarn together for a double thickness of yarn.

. . . .

- **Needles:** Size 16 circular needles: 13 US/9mm (add'l size: 9 US/5mm)
- **Accessories:** Darning needle, stitch marker, bag handle (24-inch rolled leather handle was used for Crazy Aunt Purl), plastic circle cut to size of bag bottom, or plastic take-out food container, washed and cut to size of bag bottom.

SPECIAL STITCHES:

K2togR: Knit 2 sts together so they slant to the right when viewed from RS of work (aka k2tog)

C6L: Cable 6 sts with left twist: Slip 3 sts, knit 3 sts, bring slipped sts to front of work and knit them (aka C6F: Cable 6 sts to the front).

THE RECIPE:

PART 1: BAG HEM

With a single strand of A, cast on 80 sts.

Next row (WS): Purl.

Next row (RS): Knit.

Repeat last two rows once more, four rows total.

Next row (RS): Knit, joining sts at end of round; you will be working in the round from this point on. Place a stitch marker to note start of round.

Next round (RS): Purl.

. . . .

PART 2: BAG SIDES

Continue working on the right side; set up ribbing as follows:

Round 1: (K6, P2) repeat ten times to end of round.

Rounds 2–4: Repeat round 1.

Round 5: (C6F, P2) repeat to end of round.

Round 6: Repeat round 1.

Repeat these six rounds until piece measures 9 inches or desired bag length.

TWISTED TRIM PART 1:

Turn bag inside out so that you will be working the next round on the wrong side of the work.

With A, knit 1 st. Add B by knitting 1 st with B, drop strand of B.

(Bring strand of A over dropped B strand.

With A knit 1 st, drop strand of A.

Bring strand of B over dropped A strand.

With B knit 1 st, drop strand of B.)

Repeat between parentheses around work. Your strands will become very twisted. Do NOT untwist them!

Next round: With A, purl all sts. (Hint: Slip the twists of B yarn down the strand of A to release enough A to purl the round.)

TWISTED TRIM PART 2:

(With A knit 1 st, drop strand of A.

Bring strand of B UNDER dropped A strand.

With B knit 1 st, drop strand of B.)

Bring strand of A UNDER dropped B strand.

Repeat between parentheses around all stitches. Your strands will become untwisted in this round.

Next round: With B, knit all sts. Work one more round of Twisted Trim Part 1, then break A.

Next round: With B, purl all sts. Turn work around again so that the right side of work is facing.

BAG BOTTOM:

Next round: With B (K6, k2togR) repeat to end of round—70 sts.

Next round: (K5, k2togR) repeat to end of round—60 sts.

Next round: (K4, k2togR) repeat to end of round—50 sts.

Next round: (K3, k2togR) repeat to end of round—40 sts.

Next round: (K2, k2togR) repeat to end of round—30 sts.

Next round: (K1, k2togR) repeat to end of round—20 sts.

Next round: (K2togR) repeat to end of round—10 sts.

Repeat last round once—5 sts.

Break yarn, leaving an 8-inch tail. Draw tail through remaining 5 sts; weave in end.

HEM:

Block bag by turning upside down over round canister or large can and steaming. Weave in ends.

Turn hem down at reverse stockinette stitch ridge (five rows from start of work) and sew the cast-on edge to the wrong side of the bag.

Using smaller circular needle, insert needle into every purl bump at top of work—80 purl bumps on needle.

ROLL TOP:

With B and smaller circular needle, and with right side of bag facing you, knit for 9 rounds. Bind off all sts with A. Allow the top of the bag to roll as it wants to. Weave in ends.

FINISHING:

Cut a piece of plastic or use the bottom of a plastic take-out food container that fits snugly into the purse bottom. With a darning needle, poke eight holes around the circumference of the bag, spaced evenly around. With a strand of A and working on the wrong side of the bag, tack the plastic circle in place at the first twisted float round.

Sew bag handle to top inside of bag at point where hem was turned.

ABOUT ANNIE MODESITT:

A native of Ohio, Annie taught herself to knit at age twenty-five before a move from New York City to Texas. The Texas tenure didn't last, but knitting did, and upon her return to the New York area Annie began knitting for other designers and designing for major knitting magazines. Her work has appeared in *Interweave Knits, Vogue Knitting, Knitters Magazine, Cast On, Family Circle Easy Knitting, McCalls Needlework,* and several family-oriented magazines. Author of numerous books including *Confessions of a Knitting Heretic, Knitting Millinery* and *Twist & Loop,* Annie's the inventor of the astoundingly clever Flip Knit, a low-tech, portable alternative to knitting videos. Annie knits using the Combination Method and believes that there truly is no wrong way to knit. She lives in St Paul, Minnesota, with her husband, kids, and assorted pets. Visit her online at www.anniemodesitt.com.

Acknowledgments

. . . .

Thank you to every single person who has faithfully read my online diary at crazyauntpurl.com, and laughed with me, and bawled, and agreed that the wine and potato diet isn't really all that bad. I am so grateful for you. That little website was my outlet when I had no one left to tell my dorky stories to, and I love you for listening.

This book would never have happened without Allison Janse, my fantastic editor at HCI, who pursued this idea and believed in it even when I was still nine-tenths of the way inside a bottle of cabernet. She also did not seem to mind when I called her in the middle of the night crying, or threatened to write a book called *Drunk, on Vacation, and Hopefully Covered in the Pool Boy.* She is lovely and adored.

Thank you to Lawna Oldfield for the absolutely beautiful book design and to Andrea Brower for the perfect book cover. Cheers to two obviously talented ladies.

Thank you to Terry York for "getting this" and for helping to get my book into cyberspace. Thank you to Kim Weiss for expertly spreading the word; and to everyone in sales, marketing, and production.

Thank you also to Ellen Bloom and Audrey Tawa for reaching out and introducing me to the West Hollywood knitters (and crocheters!) and to Larry Underhill for the fabulous photos. Many thanks to Annie Modesitt for her inspiration and help and general knitting awesomeness.

Finally, my deepest thank-you to my family for letting me tell your stories, too, and for making me laugh when I wanted to puddle up in the corner and eat my arm. I am forever grateful. To Jennifer, Amber, Shannon, Rebecca, Drew, and Faith—you became my family, and I love you all. Also, as family, you are stuck with me forever. And maybe the pool boy if I am lucky.

Book Club Discussion Questions

WINE SELECTION: A NICE CABERNET OR SHIRAZ

TOPIC: THE "SAFE" MARRIAGE

Laurie knew something was wrong in her marriage—she heard the late-night calls and knew her husband didn't want a baby, yet she chose to live in denial. She referred to her husband as a "safe sedan." *Are there times you denied something in your relationship? Or times you stayed with a "safe sedan"? What was the ultimate result?*

TOPIC: LIVING THE FEAR LIFE

After her husband left, Laurie isolated herself and lived what she calls the Fear Life, with the Golden Rule of being a Hermit: "I would ideally work from home, submitting my projects remotely and never attend meetings or go to an office. I would piddle in my garden and knit and talk to my cats."

Have you ever lived for a time—or in any aspect of your life—in the Fear Life? When? Why, and how did you come out of it?

TOPIC: DATING

"The predate process is exhausting. Clean your house, de-fuzz the cat hair from surfaces, tidy up, declutter as needed, vacuum, and that's just the house. There's a whole cleaning and de-fuzzing of your own self that has to happen, and here is the area where perhaps I stumbled a bit. . . ."

Does your predate process sound similar? How do you think this compares to the male gender predate process?

"You see, in my world, the world of the newly divorced and also anti-quated . . . text messaging was not part of my married life, just like flirty e-mails had never been part of the game. In other words, I was freaking clueless. And I needed to learn this text messaging *immediately.*"

Have you ever felt clueless? Has the dating landscape changed for you while you were involved with someone? Does going high-tech help or hinder you in the dating process?

TOPIC: FRIENDS

"Faith is a woman I met at my knitting group, and we had become friends, and she knew me only in the context of who I was right then. It's an odd thought that you're making friends, and they only know you as the divorced woman, never knew your husband, never knew you as a wife. It's a really liberating thought, too. You can be anyone you want to be. They see you as a whole woman, not half of a couple."

Do you have friends you lost as a result of a breakup? Are you in any way a different person "with him" than "without him," and how? Which person is more like who you really are?

TOPIC: FAMILY RULES

"There are three rules every Southern girl has hammered into her con-sciousness, and they shape you and haunt you until the day you die: Mind your manners; make the best of a situation; always wear clean panties."

Did you have any rules as part of your upbringing that still help—or haunt—you in your love/work life today?

TOPIC: WOMEN AND MONEY

"I will be the first to admit that prior to my divorce I was not the most fiscally responsible person on the planet. Whenever my financial outlook is particularly uncertain, I have the uncontrollable urge to shop. . . . [After the divorce,] I was too scared at first to even know how much debt I had. Sure, I had a pretty general idea ('general' meaning 'a whole lot of debt' and 'maybe I will cry' and 'is there any ice cream?'), but I did not know the *actual* amount. And that is sad. So once I wrote down every bill and expense and credit card, I had a full picture of my finances. . . . Taking control of my own monetary future felt like the biggest step yet on the path to self-sufficiency."

Do you share Laurie's proclivities with money? Do you feel in control of your finances or in denial? Were you raised believing it was "the man's job" to handle the money? Does it feel frightening to know the exact amount of debt you have? How and why?

TOPIC: CLOTHES

Laurie describes her postdivorce wardrobe as some of the "worst fashion choices" of her life. Sweatpants on backward and covered in cat hair and the "schlumpy 'soon-to-be-divorced woman' work uniform (black pants, unironed button-down blouse, Cardigan Of Constant Sorrow)" she wore for the better part of three months.

Do you find that what you wear embodies how you feel? Do you have any pieces of clothing you'll never throw away—or any that you've burned— because they bring back joyful or hurtful times in your life?

TOPIC: WEIGHT

"There's also something comforting about being heavier. It's no coincidence that I gained weight when I most needed some protection from the world. I wanted to minimize myself, seem smaller somehow, and what better way to become unseen than to gain weight? People's eyes pass right over you; men pay less attention to you. I wish it weren't true because it's so unfair, and yet at the same time, I used it to my advantage, building a wall of fat and insulation against the world, against rejection, against lonely."

Has your weight fluctuated in your lifetime? Do you find that the bigger you are, the less you are seen?

TOPIC: BEING GOOD TO YOURSELF

"Being good to yourself is hard work. As women, we just do for others and hope they notice. How do you put yourself first without being seen as selfish, or mean, or miserly toward others? How do you ever move your own self to the very, absolute top of all lists?"

Have you put the needs of others before your own needs? Is it selfish to make your well-being a priority? Do you worry about being perceived as selfish?

TOPIC: HOBBIES

"Strangely enough, it was knitting that rescued me from isolating myself and from becoming the crazy cat lady of my nightmares. Had I taken up stamp collecting or pottery or cross-country unicycling, I am sure I would have met equally interesting and happy people who shared my love of the newfound activity."

Are there any hobbies that rescued you at one time? Is there a hobby you'd like to try?

About the Author

Laurie Perry knits and writes in Los Angeles, where she chronicles her daily life on her online diary, Crazy Aunt Purl (www.crazyauntpurl.com). Crazy Aunt Purl has been featured in *The Wall Street Journal, The New York Times,* and on MSN.com. Perry has written for the *Los Angeles Daily News* and the *Winter Haven News Chief* in Winter Haven, Florida. Her original short story "Drunk, Divorced & Covered in Cat Hair" was published in a collection of knitting-themed essays called *Cheaper Than Therapy.* Visit her at: www.crazyauntpurl.com.

For more information,
some really cool knitting
stuff, and updates on
Laurie's misadventures,
check out:

www.crazyauntpurl.com

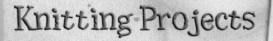

Both of these scarves were knitted in simple garter stitch using big needles. With really fuzzy yarn, it's easier to hide wine-inspired mistakes.

This is me wearing all of my knitted crap, on the same day —in L.A.

Magic Scarf

I love self-striping yarn, and I tend to buy it in bulk. Unlike husbands, when it comes to yarn we can buy as many skeins as possible and seal them away in Ziploc bags until we find a use for them.

1

Work in Progress

Bob patrols this scarf for intruders.

Giant Pom-Pom Scarf

This giganto-long scarf started life as a swatch, but the yarn was so darn pretty that I just kept going. These giant pom-poms can be used as weapons if necessary.

2

Hats are superfast! I'm a painfully slow knitter, and even I can make a hat in a day. If you use variegated or self-striping yarn, it will look like you put far more effort into the hat than you really did.

Look how cute my dad and my brother Eric are posing for this picture. It was only eleventy hundred degrees outside in Florida when they modeled these hats. Afterward, I believe someone fainted. Nothing like wool hats at the height of summer!

Cat Tunnel

Nothing says "Hot Divorcee" more than a gigantic hand-knitted cat toy. I mean really.

Do you think the man in the cement and lumber aisle at the home improvement store had any idea this cardboard tube would become a cat toy?

Yes, one of my cats thinks he's a dog. Maybe we all need therapy.

"I'm too sexy for my hat, too sexy for my hat."

I have reached the exact age when all of my girlfriends are getting knocked up at the same time. Everywhere I turn, it seems someone else is having a baby. This is the perfect not-baby-pink-and-blue gift for any expectant mom with a sense of humor. Sara Neff created this shaped blankie with an attached horned hood. Just perfect for those days when junior is being anything but an angel . . .

5

Felted Bracelet Bags

This bag will shrink a lot when it's felted—mine was almost half this size when finished. Make sure your final knitted bag will be long enough for your lipstick and cell phone before you start the decreases.

Yes, at first it will look like you're knitting a thong.

Attach the handle and decorate to your heart's content, with jewelry or Allison Sanka's Stashbuster Knitted Flower.